COME WITH ME THROUGH JUDE

Come with me through
JUDE

David Pawson

Shalom!

J. David Pawson

Anchor Recordings

First published in Great Britain 2012
by
Anchor Recordings Ltd
72 The Street
Kennington
Ashford
TN24 9HS UK

ISBN 978-0-9569376-2-9

Printed in Great Britain by Imprint Digital, Exeter
Printed in USA by CreateSpace.com

Contents

This book is based on a series of talks. Originating as it does from the spoken word, its style will be found by many readers to be somewhat different from my usual written style. It is hoped that this will not detract from the substance of the biblical teaching found here.

The outline provided below is intended to help with the reading, and was not necessarily fully followed in the talks.

As always, I ask the reader to compare everything I say or write with what is written in the Bible and, if at any point a conflict is found, always to rely upon the clear teaching of scripture.

David Pawson

THE LETTER OF JUDE

In what follows, when I refer to the text of Jude I am using my own translation in which I have tried as honestly as I can to bring out every little bit of the meaning in the language in which it was written.

¹This letter comes from Judas, Jude for short, one of the slaves bought by King Jesus and the younger brother of the James you all know. It is addressed to those who have been called out of the world who are now loved, one in God the Father's family, and who are being kept for presentation to King Jesus. ²May you experience all you can hold of his mercy, peace and love, which you've already received.

³Loved ones, I was fully intending to correspond with you about the wonderful salvation we share but found I had to write quite a different kind of letter, urging you to keep up the painful struggle for the true faith which was delivered to the early saints once and for all. ⁴For I have heard that certain persons who shall be nameless have sneaked in among you, godless men of the sort whose doom was recorded long ago. They twist the free grace of God into an excuse for blatant immorality and deny that King Jesus is our only Master and Lord. Now I want to remind you of some of those absolute truths which you already know perfectly well, especially that God is not the kind of God to be trifled with.

⁵You will recall that though the Lord brought a whole nation safely out of Egypt he subsequently exterminated them all because they wouldn't trust him. ⁶Nor were his angels any more exempt than his people, and when some of them deserted their rank and abandoned their proper station he took them into custody and is keeping them permanently chained in the lowest and darkest dungeon until their trial on the great day of judgment. ⁷Like Sodom and Gomorrah, together with their two neighbouring towns, they glutted themselves with gross debauchery, craving for abnormal intercourse just as the angels had done. And the fate they suffered in the fire that burned for ages is a solemn warning to us all.

⁸In spite of these precedents in history, the people who have wormed their way into your fellowship pollute their own bodies in exactly the same manner, belittle divine authority and smear angels in glory. ⁹Why even the chief of all the angels, Michael, whose name means godlike, did not dare to accuse Satan directly of blasphemy when they were arguing about who owned the body of Moses. He was content to leave judgment in God's hands and simply said, "The Lord reprimand you." ¹⁰Yet these men among you don't hesitate to malign whatever they don't understand. And the things they do understand will prove their undoing in the end, for all their knowledge of life comes from their animal instincts like brute beasts without the capacity for reason.

[11]Woe betide them. They have gone down the same road as Cain. They have rushed headlong into the same blunder as Balaam, and from the same motive, money. They come to the same doom as Korah did in his abortive rebellion. [12]These people have the cheek to sit and eat with you at your loving fellowship meals, though they are only looking for pasture for themselves. Like submerged rocks, they could wreck everything. They are like clouds driven so hard by the wind they drop no rain. They are like uprooted trees in the autumn with neither leaves nor fruit —dead as dead. [13]They are like wild waves of the sea stirring up the filthy foam of shame. They are like shooting stars leaving their orbits, destined to disappear into a black hole forever.

[14]Enoch, who lived only seven generations after the first man, Adam, saw all this coming and knew that God would do something about it. He was referring to these very people when he made his prophetic proclamation: 'Look out, the Lord has arrived with ten thousand of his angels [15]to put all human beings in the dark and convict all godless people of all the godless deeds they have committed in their godless lives, and of all the harsh words these godless sinners have spoken against him.' [16]The speech of these people gives them away. They are discontented grumblers, always complaining and finding fault. Their mouths are full of swollen opinions

about themselves but they are happy to flatter others if it is to their advantage.

[17]Now, loved ones, you should have remembered what the apostles of our Lord Jesus Christ said would happen. [18]They predicted that in the final age there are bound to be those who pour scorn on godliness, whose lives will be totally governed by their own godless appetites. [19]People like this only create divisions among you since they go by the instincts of their flesh and know nothing of the inspiration of the Spirit.

[20]As for you loved ones, be sure to go on building yourselves up on the solid foundation of the faith that leads to holiness, continually praying in the way the Holy Spirit gives you.

[21]Stay in love with God while you wait patiently for the day when our Lord Jesus Christ in his sheer mercy brings us into living immortality. [22]Regarding the others, here is my advice. To those who are still wavering between truth and error, be especially kind and gentle as you argue with them. [23]And those who have allowed themselves to be misled must be snatched from the flames before they are badly burnt, and even those who have been thoroughly contaminated must be treated better than they deserve, though you must never lose your fear of being infected by them even through their stained underwear. [24]Above all there is one person who is able to keep you from falling into this error and to stand you upright in his glorious presence without any imperfection but with great jubilation. [25]He is the

only God there is and he is our Saviour too, through Jesus Christ our Lord. To him alone belong all the glory, all the majesty, all the power and all the authority in the universe. They belonged to him before history began, they belong to him now in this present time and they will belong to him for all ages to come. Amen.

ANALYTICAL OUTLINE

INTRODUCTION – a neglected letter (1-2) p. 17

A. LEARNING FROM THE PAST (3-19) p. 69

1.THEIR CORRUPTION

2.THEIR CONDEMNATION

a. CREED (3-4)
i. Grace – licence for immorality.
ii. Christ – lordship denied.

a. RETRIBUTION (5-7)
i. Exodus generation.
ii. Fallen angels.

b. CONDUCT (8)
i. Pollute own bodies.
ii. Reject authority.
iii. Slander angels.

iii. Sodom and Gomorrah.
(scripture)

b. RESPECT (9)
i. Archangel Michael.

c. COGITATION (10)
i. Don't understand, so abuse.
ii. Do understand, like animals.

ii. Devil.
(tradition)

c. REBELLION (11)
i. Cain.
ii. Balaam.
iii. Korah.

d. CHARACTER (12-13)
i. Fleeting clouds – drought.
ii. Fruitless trees – death.
iii. Foaming waves – debris.
iv. Falling stars – darkness.

(scripture)

d. REVELATION (14-15)
i. Enoch's prophecy.
ii. Coming judgement.
(tradition)

e. CONVERSATION (16)
i. Grumblers, faultfinders.
ii. Follow own desires.
iii. Boast about themselves.
iv. Flatter for advantage.

e. RIDICULE (17-18)
i. Apostle's warning.
ii. Scoffers.
(scripture)

f. COMPULSION (19)
i. Divisive.
ii. Follow natural instincts.
iii. Do not have the Spirit.

B. LIVING IN THE PRESENT (20-23) p. 137

1. YOURSELVES (20-21)
a. Edification.
b. Petition.
c. Submission.

2. OTHERS (23)
a. Wavering.
b. Wayward.
c. Wicked.

C. LOOKING TO THE FUTURE (24-25) p. 147

1. THE ABLE GOD (24)
a. To prevent you falling.
b. To present you faultless.

2. THE ONLY GOD (25)
a. His sovereignty.
b. His eternity.

x Pg 18 – The Lost Book of Enoch
by David Humphreys

1

A NEGLECTED LETTER
Read 1–4

Why has the letter of Jude been so neglected? Very few people quote from it except for the last two verses, which we rather like. You might think the reason is simply that it is a little book, and we tend to overlook small things. So often we think that big is beautiful — the biggest crowd, the biggest meeting. But God does not think that way. He looks for quality, not quantity. Incidentally, we need to remember this when we are praying. He said that you will not be heard for much speaking. It is how deep your prayer, not how long it is, that gets through to God. God does not look for size. Little things can be very valuable to him. Little books of the Bible are just as valuable to God as the big books, and they should be to you. Haggai, Zechariah, Habakkuk and Jonah are termed 'minor' prophets, yet they were big men to God —they had a big message. We should never think that because a book in the Bible is short, it is not as important as the others. However, I do not think that can be the real reason why people neglect Jude, because 2 John and 3 John are smaller yet not so neglected.

The second reason could be that Jude is a strange book. It refers to things about which we know little or nothing, and interest is related to knowledge. If you know something about a subject then you are interested in more of it, but if you do not know much about a thing, you are probably much less interested. If I were to give you a lecture on computers (which I couldn't!) you would be fascinated if you already knew a bit about computing, but much less so if you knew nothing about it. The fact is that when we read this strange book of Jude, we discover that it refers to things of which most of us know very little. It mentions Michael the Archangel arguing with Satan as to who owned the body of Moses. Did you ever think about that? Did you ever wonder why they argued about it? You probably never even knew that when Moses died, Michael the Archangel and Satan had a big argument about who was to conduct the funeral! If an issue seems obscure to you, then you are probably not all that interested. And there are other strange things in this book — like angels having sex with human beings. Such ideas are beyond our imagination, though they sometimes come back into fashion in films. It is curious that the world is getting back to ideas which to Christians are strange concepts. Jude talks about people about whom we have a vague idea but not much knowledge. Balaam, for example. You have probably heard of Balaam's ass —

and Balaam finally listened to his ass, which is quite a wise thing to do if the ass is telling you the will of God — but that is about all we know about Balaam! We need to know much more. Or what about Korah? Do you know what that is about? Probably not, yet Jude is building quite a lot on the story of Korah's rebellion. So, because it is full of strange ideas and strange things which we have not really thought about, we don't really take to Jude with a great deal of interest, and that is a mistake. We need to know about everything in the Bible, if we are going to be filled with the knowledge of God.

Here is a third reason, related to the previous one. Where did Jude get all these curious stories? Where is he quoting from? Is he quoting from the Old Testament? There is nothing in the Old Testament about an argument over the body of Moses. The answer is that he is getting it from books written in the four centuries between the Old Testament and the New Testament. When there were no prophets there were still books being written and we call them the Apocrypha, which means 'hidden'. These books do not appear in Protestant Bibles. The Apocrypha consists of books like the book of Enoch and the book called the Assumption of Moses. Or there is a book called Ecclesiasticus (not Ecclesiastes!) which is quoted at Remembrance Day Services in November — but you probably did not know that when you heard the quote. Here is Jude quoting from books that are not in our Protestant Bibles, though Roman Catholics would recognise them.

Why are they not in our Bibles? For a very simple reason: we do not believe they are the word of God. Not once in any of those books written between Malachi and Matthew does there come the phrase which occurs 3,808 times in our Old Testament: 'Thus says the Lord'. So we do not believe they are God speaking to us. But that does not mean that what they contain is not true. There is truth to be found outside the Bible. Other people have said true things that we need to hear and take note of. Other apostles, like Paul, freely quoted from the Greek poets when the Greek poets said something true. From one point of view the Bible does not have a monopoly of truth, other people have said true things. Shakespeare said some true things. And providing it is true, you can quote it. And Jude is not building any doctrine on these quotations from the Apocrypha, he is using them as illustrations because some of the things in those books are true. So if the Holy Spirit guided Jude to quote from them, then the Holy Spirit knew that what he was quoting was true. So never assume that the only source of truth is the Bible, but you can check whether anything else you hear is true by checking it with the Bible. If it lines up with the Bible, it is true, and if it doesn't, it is not. So Christians have often been a little suspicious of Jude and observed that he quotes from the Apocrypha. This suspicion has been widespread, and some neglect this book for this reason. But I still do not think that is the main reason for neglect of this letter.

The fourth possible reason for the neglect of Jude is that it is a very severe book. It is stern, serious and sombre, and we like to be cheered up. We want to read our Bible and feel better after we have read it. We want to be able to rejoice after we have heard the word of God. We want to be uplifted; there is so much in the world to depress us that we want the Bible to encourage us. Indeed there is a mood abroad, even among Christians, that we must not say anything negative: accentuate the positive; the power of positive thinking; don't ever say anything negative from your mouth.

However, we want to hear what is right, not what is wrong. Here in the word of God is a letter that is negative almost from beginning to end. Why? Because we live in a day when it is not just important to say what is true, it is also important to tell people about what is false. But the cardinal virtue of the age in which we live is tolerance. 'Don't ever tell anybody they're wrong. Tell everybody they're right. Be like Alice in Wonderland —we will all win and we will all have prizes. All roads lead to God. It does not matter what you really believe, as long as you are sincere.' That mood of our age has infected Christians. But unless we are willing, like Jude, to say 'that is wrong', as well as 'that is right'— 'this is true, but that is false' — we are going to lose the battle for the faith once delivered to the saints, and we will be to blame. For I want to show you that the real battle going on in Britain is not outside the church, it is inside the church. The letter of

Jude tells us what that battle is.

You may think we are losing the battle in Britain because things are happening out there in our nation and legislation has been and is being passed in our Parliament. But that is not where the battle is being lost. The Lord has laid heavily on my spirit that the church is losing the battle *within its own ranks* in this country, and the reason why we are losing the battle outside of us is because we are losing the battle inside. We are not fighting on the true front. That is my burden.

So I make no apology for teaching on this very serious letter: a negative, stern, rebuking letter, and yet a letter which is necessary. We cannot praise the only God our Saviour until we face the truth first.

The fifth possible reason for the neglect of Jude's letter is because it is sharp. It cuts. I was rummaging around in my sponge bag one day and plunged my hand in, and there was a razor without a guard on it. I sliced right through the end of my finger. For a while the wound kept opening, and it was very painful. It stung. It was sharp. I sucked it hard but it still stung when I would catch it on something and open it up. It was cut with a sharp edge — and the little letter of Jude has a sharp cutting edge which exposes raw flesh.

That indeed is the real problem: flesh in the church. This little letter will cut through that and expose it, and that is going to sting. But we are sensitive, and the real reason that we neglect a passage of scripture is that we do not like it. Recalling childhood days, I think of children at a party seeing a pile of jam sandwiches, and before you could stop them they picked the sandwiches up, opened them out and licked the jam, putting the bread back on the plate! Deep down, we can be like that. That is how people read their Bible if they are not careful. Some even used to buy a thing like a chocolate box which was full of rolled-up promises, and pick them out and read one every day. Very rarely in those promise boxes are there conditions attached to the promise printed on the piece of paper. We lick the jam out . . . . Take an example: Jesus said, 'Lo, I am with you always'. Do you want to put that up on your wall? Lovely text! But there is a condition attached to it. The whole sentence says: 'Go and make disciples . . .' and, 'Lo, I am with you . . .' —and you will not get the 'Lo . .' until you have the 'Go . . . !' Our favourite passages are the nice sweet ones. But we need the bread. The whole thing is a balanced diet. We need the fibre to give us strength.

So the real reason for the neglect of Jude is that it is sharp. But let me tell you, whenever you feel the sharp edge of God's word, it is the sharpness of a surgeon's knife. God's word is like so many things. James, the brother of the writer of this letter, said that it is like a mirror. You look into it and who do you see? Yourself. Some people do not like that, so they go away and forget what they saw. But the word of God is also like a two-edged sword. Roman soldiers had a long, thin sword which they used when they wanted to fight one-to-one, fencing, but they had a short sword, shaped like an old hay-knife or a spade, very sharp, very heavy, with a ridge down the middle. One soldier could hold off a hundred men with that. He would swing it from side to side and, given its weight, nothing could stop it. If the soldier swung it round quickly, people could not get near him, it would slice their arms and legs off.

That was a sharp two-edged sword, and the word of God is like that. You can slay hundreds with it. And it is exactly the shape of a tongue. When, in the book of Revelation, John saw Jesus, he saw that his tongue was like a two-edged sword — and seven churches felt the edge of that tongue very soon after that. But it is to get the cancer out. And my burden is that there is a cancer in the body of Christ in the land in which I live. There is a very dangerous growth taking place, not just among the dead churches but among the most lively churches, the most Spirit-filled churches. There is something happening that Jude's knife will expose and, praise God, cut out.

You see, every Christian must live dangerously. This world is not a safe place for Christians. We are living in enemy-occupied territory, so it is the most dangerous thing to be part of the church. We are called to live dangerously because this is Satan's world. We know we are of God, but we also know that the whole world lies in the grip of the evil one. Part of the danger is external, and part is internal. The external part belongs to what we call persecution. My wife and I have been to parts of the world (both in the East and in parts of Europe) where the church is under very great pressure. Moreover, Jesus promised that before his return his church would be persecuted in every nation. There are many countries in the world where Christians are persecuted, and the number is increasing. Whilst in the United Kingdom more of us now suffer social embarrassment and some verbal abuse, there are no secret police in our meetings to report and there is nobody waiting outside church to take your name down, so that your children may be kept out of university because you are a Christian. Nevertheless, it is getting very tough for some of those who convert from another religion, and recent legislation has created extremely serious difficulties for people in some jobs (such as Christian registrars, nurses, others in the caring professions, guest house proprietors and indeed any who are willing to be known as Christians in their workplaces), as well as for those who undertake Christian evangelism in public and run the risk of being arrested out on the streets for exercising what used to be regarded as a basic civil liberty.

But the church is never destroyed by outside pressure. In fact the opposite happens. We visited a church where the people coming to its meetings were told that they would be fined 10% of their wages for three months for attending. That was in a country where it takes a day and a half's wages to buy a pound of meat; where they are not allowed to heat their homes properly in the depths of winter, they are not allowed to have more than a forty watt light bulb in their home; if they have a car they are only allowed five litres of petrol per month, and bread is not allowed to be sold on the day it is baked, it has to be kept for two or three days until it is as hard as rock before it can be sold. Yet in that place we found that there were two and a half thousand people trying to get into a building that would hold about fifteen hundred!

Wherever the church faces external danger, it grows. In the first three hundred years of Christianity they were not allowed to build any buildings, they were thrown to the lions; mothers had their babies taken from them and were told, 'You cannot have your baby back unless you deny Christ.' And they refused to do so. The church never grew so fast as in those years of Roman persecution.

I visited the People's Republic of China at a time when some five million people belonged to the official church, the 'Three Self Movement', but an estimated forty-five million had come to Christ through house churches in a few years. People were saying: Isn't it marvellous that China is opening up again? I would reply, 'No, it's terrible. I just hope missionaries will not be able to get in and spoil it. The only reason I am glad the "bamboo curtain" is lifting is because the Chinese might be able to come and tell us how to do it.'

The answer lies in external danger. I was having lunch with a Presbyterian pastor and he was telling me about his church. He described the biggest ever meetings of Christians — nearly three million at one meeting. He told me about his own church of 25,000 members when I asked, 'What's the secret of your growth?' (It was in South Korea as you might have guessed.)

He replied, 'Prayer is the secret. Our people meet at five o'clock every morning to pray.'

'No, that's not the secret,' I responded. 'What is it?'

'Well, that's what we think it is and that's what we always say it is —prayer.'

Then I re-phrased the question: 'Tell me, what makes people pray at five o'clock in the morning? Then you will have told me the secret. It's not a technique of holding five o'clock prayer meetings; it is what *makes* people get up and pray. Tell me when the prayer started in your church.'

He pondered that, and then answered: 'Well, I'll have to think back. Oh, I remember. We are nine miles from the North Korean border, and the North Koreans dig tunnels underneath the barbed wire and come through and terrorise us. Our pastor, his wife and mother lived in the house near the church, and one night North Koreans who had burrowed under the boundary came into the house and lined the three of them up. They said to the pastor, "Deny Christ or we'll kill your mother." He refused, so they shot his mother dead. Then they said, "Deny Christ or we'll kill your wife." Again he refused, so they shot his wife dead. Here was this pastor, holding the hands of his dead wife and his mother. Then they said, "Deny Christ or we'll kill you." He still refused. So they put a gun to his head and pulled the trigger.

But the gun jammed and wouldn't fire — and they ran.' My friend continued, 'Come to think of it, that was the week we started the prayer meetings.'

'Now,' I said, 'you've told me the secret. Now I know.'

But we in England are not living nine miles from the border. We are not under that kind of pressure and life is easier for us. But I want to tell you very solemnly you had better start getting ready for persecution, because it is on its way. Pressure from outside the church only makes it grow. The blood of the martyrs is the seed of the church, and there are two thousand years of church history to prove it. There has not been one period of ten years in the last two thousand years when there have not been martyrs for Jesus Christ. Whenever I hear speakers say: 'Do you want to be wealthy? Do you want to be healthy? Do you want to be safe? — Just have faith', I want to read these words to them: 'By faith they wandered destitute. By faith they lived in caves and holes in the ground. Some women received their dead raised to life again but others were killed with the sword. Some were sawn asunder.' So by faith they were destitute, wandered around homeless or killed! That is the life of faith that I read about in the Bible. It is rather pathetic when you meet people who are trying to get as comfortable and wealthy and healthy as possible by faith. Faith is something much, much deeper than that. It is a faith in God, a faith such as Shadrach, Meschach and Abednego had — you can throw us in the fiery furnace and our God can save us, but even if he doesn't, we won't bow down to your God.

The church can never be destroyed from outside. The more persecution that comes, the stronger we shall be. The more we are attacked from outside, the purer we shall be, the more we shall stand together. You cannot afford the luxury of division and denominational labels when you are under persecution. I remember having a meal in our home with Helen Roseveare, the doctor among rebels in Zaire. I remember her saying this: 'When you are being raped on the same bed as a Roman Catholic nun, you don't discuss denominations. You cry to the same Jesus.'

But now let us turn from the 'outside' to the 'inside', because the church can be destroyed from inside; it is not external dangers, it is internal dangers we need to be concerned about, and this is Jude's concern. The devil doesn't really believe that persecution will do anything but good to us. But he does know that Christian joy and peace and fellowship and love can be destroyed from inside. There are in fact two great dangers that can destroy the church from the inside: legalism that is too strict and too narrow-minded, and a liberalism that is too lax and too broad-minded, making her helpless in the face of a nation that desperately needs God's salvation. Legalism is the 'Pharisee', liberalism is the 'Sadducee' and neither of them like Jesus at all. Pharisees plotted to kill Jesus and the Sadducees achieved it. But they were totally different. The Pharisees were strict, the legalists, and Jesus was much too free for them; the Sadducees were lax, they did not mind how they made their money or how they got power, and they were, above all, freely into divorce and remarriage. They did not like Jesus either, because he was a threat. The legalists and the liberals of his day combined to crucify our Lord Jesus Christ. Ever since then we have been facing these two dangers. Legalism is making rules for other people, imposing standards on them from the outside so that they can perform outwardly when their heart may not be in it at all. We all do this. We conform in clothes. I am free in Christ to wear a tie and a suit to a meeting (as is my custom), and I do not have to conform to jeans. I am free! How we make rules for each other! 'Oh, we don't dance in our church.' 'We don't drink in this church.' 'We don't wear make-up in our church.' We don't do this, we don't do that . . . . Legalism! If the Holy Spirit tells you not to do a thing, of course that is quite another matter.

A boy called Dan came to our church. He had been rather a rough lad but he got converted, and from then on he came to worship every Sunday morning, and every Sunday evening he went to the cinema — whatever was showing. After a few weeks he came to me and asked, 'David, should a Christian go to the cinema every Sunday evening?'

I replied, 'I'm not going to tell you.'

Could you have resisted telling him? But he said he wanted to know and I said to him that he had better ask

Jesus. He continued, 'Well, how do I find out from him?'

'Take him with you next Sunday night and see if he enjoys it,' I advised.

So he went along to the local cinema, and to the girl at the box office he said, 'Two tickets, please.'

She looked around, and seeing nobody else said, 'Is your girlfriend joining you?'

'No,' he replied, 'It's alright, two tickets please.'

'Well,' she said, 'who's the other ticket for?'

'Jesus,' came the answer.

She was so scared by this that she phoned the manager. The manager came and asked what the trouble was. 'He wants two tickets. I've given him two tickets, but he wants one of them for Jesus,' she said.

Then the manager began to stutter and stammer. 'Well, if he wants two tickets, that's business for us, it's not up to us to ask . . . . Let him have two tickets.'

So Dan went in and he sat down, and he said, 'Jesus you sit there, I'll sit here.' Ten minutes into the film he said, 'Are you enjoying it?' Two minutes later he was out of the cinema! That is the liberty of the Spirit.

How easily we make rules which are traditions of men rather than the word of God. We have all done it. We impose a standard of behaviour on people from the outside — and the tragedy of it is that they conform, though their heart may be a long way away, and indeed the Pharisee does not usually get the inside cleaned up.

A mother said to a little boy, 'Sit down.' And he didn't. So she said again, 'Sit down.' Still he didn't.

So she lifted her hand. She said, 'Sit down or I'll . . .'
—and he sat down. Then he muttered under his breath,
'The outside of me is sitting down, but the inside is still
standing up.' That is what legalism produces, and it
kills the spirit. I have been to fellowships where there
is a spirit of legalism and the glory has departed. The
people are conforming, but it is dead.

But it is the other danger that is the more prominent
now — the danger of liberalism, becoming too broad-
minded and lax, too casual. This was brought home to
me very forcibly some years ago when a friend of ours
from a communist country was visiting. He went to a
church in England which had a reputation for being
evangelical and charismatic, and our pastor friend was
shocked to the core of his being. There was no fear of
God in the place. The service was led by a woman who
was not just immodestly but indecently dressed; the
pastor's own marriage had broken up, and the whole
event was so casual. Now, if anything, the Christians
in his home country tended to the legalistic side (I say
that in love, it would be their temptation), but he saw
a liberalism of behaviour in the church here, and it
shocked him that people could be so casual with God.
I was ashamed that he should have seen that here, but
I know it was not an isolated case.

One day I was lying in the bath, meditating. (Do you
do that? It is an ideal place.) I was engaging in what
I call interrogatory prayer, which means asking God
questions. I find that he answers when you ask. I said,

'Lord, there's something missing in the churches of Britain, there's something missing even from the finest churches in Britain, and I can't put my finger on it. I know it's not there. But I don't know what it is. What is the missing dimension?' He answered and I rather wished he hadn't. He said, 'The fear of God.'

When fear of God becomes a phobia, it develops into legalism, but when the fear of God is absent then liberalism takes over. By 'liberalism' I am not only referring to a bishop denying the Virgin birth and the physical resurrection, but the liberalism that lowers Christ's standards. Let me take one example from the Bible. Jesus' standard in relation to marriage was this, and he made it absolutely clear: whoever divorces and remarries is committing adultery; and whoever marries a divorcee is committing adultery. That was his plain teaching, but it is not the standard by which the church is now governing itself. Liberalism is not just something related to theology and doctrine, it is something related to ethics and behaviour. When our belief is liberalised, our behaviour will be liberalised. When our theology becomes sentimental our ethics become situational. In case you do not know what I mean by that, situational ethics holds, for example, that it is not always wrong to have sex before marriage. The circumstances (the situation) must be taken into account. In this way there has been a liberalising of behaviour as well as of belief. If legalism will strangle a church, the effect of liberalism is that the power will leave, slowly but surely, until one day the church will find itself like Samson who did not realise that the Lord had left him.

That is my burden. We can still learn from Jude, who was actually one of the brothers of Jesus and lived with him during those years. He thought Jesus was crazy until he rose from the dead. We are told that Jude became a missionary, and he went out to speak the truth. It is from that man, the third brother down from Jesus, son of Joseph and Mary, that we have this word.

I have a strong feeling that too many of us in this country are playing games with God, we are playing church, and that is my burden. You will recall that though the Lord brought a whole nation safely out of Egypt he subsequently exterminated them all because they would not trust him enough. Nor were his angels any more exempt than his people. When some of them deserted their rank and abandoned their proper station, he took them into custody and is keeping them permanently chained in the lowest and darkest dungeon until their trial on the great day of judgment. Likewise Sodom and Gomorrah, together with their two neighbouring towns, glutted themselves with gross debauchery, craving for abnormal intercourse just as the angels had done, and the fate they suffered in the fire that burned for ages is a solemn warning to us all. I want to begin by reminding you that this letter is not a theological paper but a real letter from a real person to real people.

We have begun to look at what is written on the

envelope, but they did not put letters in envelopes in those days, they wrote the letter on a long strip of paper and rolled it up, and as you unrolled the first bit they had four things right at the top of the roll. They would first of all put the name of the person sending it. How sensible — every letter I get, I have to look at the end to find out who it is from, unless I recognise the handwriting. What a silly custom it is to put your name right at the end! Some people writing from overseas put their name on the back of the envelope and you know who it has come from, and that is helpful. They were much more sensible in those days: firstly, they wrote who it was from, and secondly, they wrote who it was to. Thirdly, they would write a greeting to wish the reader well, and fourthly, they put down the reason for writing. What a sensible format, and letters in the New Testament provide that information.

First of all, it is from Judas, yet ever since, even though he wrote 'Judas', Christians have called him 'Jude' for short. Why? Because the name 'Judas' has such evil associations that we do not want it. There was a famous artist who once painted a picture of the Last Supper. It took him some years, and he searched everywhere for a man whose face was pure enough to model for Jesus. He found a man who had one of those lovely open faces, and he painted him in the centre. But for years he could not find a man whose face was subtly evil enough to model for Judas. Years later he found such a man and asked, 'Would you model for me please, I'm an artist.' The man agreed, and he sat while the artist painted Judas. While the artist was painting, the man said, 'You know, it's not the first time I've been in this studio. You employed me years ago.' It was the same man. What a warning! Judas was a man who preached the gospel, healed the sick, exorcised demons and finished in hell. So we do not like to use the name of this man and we just call him Jude. But he wrote, 'This is from Judas.' There are five people called Judas in the scripture and it is a common name, the same as the word 'Judah', which means 'Praise God'. So which one is this? He says: 'It is the brother of James, the James you all know.' What a humble man. Who was the James they all knew? The elder at Jerusalem. Who was he? He was the actual brother of Jesus. So why did he not say: 'I am a brother of Jesus'? He just says, in effect: I am second fiddle to my brother James. What a lovely man! He can say to Jesus: I am one of the slaves you bought. I get to like Jude as soon as I read his name, a man who is quite content to say: I am the brother of my brother and I am a slave to the other one. That is his attitude. He is not standing on ceremony. Some people might have written: I am one of Jesus' brothers and James is my brother.

Of the brother Jesus, whom he had lived with in the carpenter's home in Nazareth for so many years, he says he is now his slave, Jesus bought him — yet this man had said of Jesus that he was crazy. There was a time when Jesus' mother and brothers and sisters came to put him away because they said he was beside himself, which was their way of saying 'schizophrenic' — that he had two personalities, one who thought he was the Messiah. People came to put him away and said, 'Jesus, your brothers are outside and your mother.' But Jesus said, 'My brothers, my mother . . . anyone who does the will of my Father is my brother.' So James was not truly his brother at that stage, nor later when we are told that the brothers of Jesus did not believe in Jesus. Then everybody was expecting the Messiah to appear at the Feast of Tabernacles — and why did he not go up to the feast and do a few miracles if he thought he was the Messiah? Jesus had to say to his own brothers: 'My time has not come yet' — and he went up secretly, halfway through the feast.

Judas and James were two of those brothers, and even at the cross they still were not believers in Jesus, their own brother, and so the result was that Jesus entrusted his mother to someone else outside the family. Did you ever notice that? He would not trust his own brothers with his mother! He said: John, look after my mum. But, some time after the resurrection, the brothers of Jesus believed in him. He actually appeared to them.

Jesus got five out of his twelve apostles from amongst his own family relatives. Did you know that? That is why they were invited to the wedding at Cana. All his four brothers: James, Joses, Judas who came next, and Simon, the youngest. So Mary's other four boys all became missionaries for Jesus. They are listed in the

New Testament. Isn't it exciting that Jesus' own family, those who knew him best, came to believe in him?

So we have a letter in our hands from someone as close to the Lord Jesus as that, yet he would only say, 'I'm his slave now.' He was only a half-brother of course, because Joseph was not the father of Jesus as he was of Judas and James, but they had the same mother. Now he says that he is Jesus' slave. What a change!

To whom is Jude writing? The address is without a name, but it must be a specific church because it is a specific problem that he has heard about. He is too sensitive to give the name of the church, so he puts it in general terms, which enables us to receive this letter. He says, 'I am writing to those who are called and those who are loved and those who are kept' — so if you can apply those three words to yourself then this letter is to you. But if you are not called and not loved and not kept, then you might as well not read on any further because it is not for you.

I am assuming that you have heard the call of the Lord and responded, so the letter is to you — you are called, and it was God who chose you, you did not choose him. I used to think that I chose God, but looking back now I realise he chose me —because he did the calling. I just answered, and I realised I did not answer when the first call came. I am amazed at the patience of God. A Scottish engineer came to me once and said, 'David, in the middle of World War II, my mates were all being killed around me and I said: "God, if you'll get me back to my family safely I'll go to church for the rest of my life — I'll really try and live a good life.'" He escaped from that battle, one of the few who got out alive, and he came back but he never kept his promise. He came to see me once, and he said, 'David, can you have a second bite at the cherry?'

'Of course you can,' I replied, 'because you wouldn't have come and asked that unless God was still calling you' — and he came the second time.

'Called', and 'loved' — that is a most beautiful word. It does not say loved *by* God, it says loved *in* God. I like that little word 'in'. You are not just loved by God you are loved right into him, you are in his love, you are living it. What is your address? Mine is 'in Christ'. That will find me anywhere now; it is where I live. I remember meeting a German pastor and he said that once in his young days, before he was a Christian, he had joined Hitler Youth, and he stood in front of the German flag with the swastika, and the officer in charge said to him, 'Where do you live?'

'I live in Hamburg,' he replied.

'Wrong answer, where do you live?'

'I live in Germany.'

'Wrong answer, where do you live?'

'I live in the Third Reich.'

'Wrong answer, where do you live?'

'I don't know what you want me to say.'

And the officer said: 'Say, "I live in Hitler."'

Years later that German pastor said to me, 'I've

changed my address, I now live in Christ.'

We are loved in God, right into him, and the third address here is your full address: called, loved, *kept*. And not kept *by* Jesus, kept *for* Jesus. Again, the little words are so important in the Bible. Consider this sentence: 'She's going to be a grandmother in a month, she's already keeping things in a bottom drawer, little woolly things, she can't wait to be a grandmother for the first time, she's keeping things for the baby.' The point is you are being kept not for *you* but for Jesus.

Now that is the address; does it apply to you? If so, then read the rest of the letter. If it does not apply to you, do not rest until it does, I beg you. Make sure you are called and loved and kept.

But none of these things means that you are *safe*, and I want you to know this. I wish people would stop thinking that they are safe once they are called, loved and kept. The expression 'once saved, always saved' is sometimes used, and what people really mean is: 'once safe, always safe' and that is a dangerous thing. You will not be safe until you are dead. That is my message to you, because all those three things demand a response. You are *called*, but that does not make you safe unless you come and you go on coming when you are called. And I find the Lord goes on calling, he does not stop calling. *Loved* —that is calling for a response of love. *Kept* — that also is calling for a response of keeping yourself. Never take half the Bible truth, it is unsafe to do so. The same Paul who said, 'I am persuaded that he is able to keep what I've committed', said in the same letter, 'I have kept faith with him.' And this very letter says: 'You are kept' and 'keep yourselves in the love of God'. There are two sides to truth, so often we must hold them together in tension.

A great Christian was asked to write his auto-biography, and he said, 'No, someone else must write my biography.' When asked why, he said, 'Because I have seen too many men fall in the last lap.' John Bunyan, in *The Pilgrim's Progress*, says that he saw, even at the pearly gates of heaven, there was a road that led to hell. This is something in that famous book which some Christians do not like. But as I have already pointed out, you are not safe, you are in enemy occupied territory, and a Christian is living dangerously. Even when we are surrounded by Christians, there are dangers we need to be aware of. And that is why Jude writes the letter.

We are going to see in one of the examples he brings to us that of all those who came out of Egypt, who had been under the blood of the lamb, who had come through the Red Sea, only two got to Canaan. That, says Jude, is an example and a warning to us. Paul, in 1 Corinthians 10, uses exactly the same incident to warn us that what happened to people under the old covenant can happen to people under the new covenant as well. So never have a false sense of security; don't ever build that security on half the texts in the New Testament. There are warnings of those who have shipwrecked their faith, those who did not keep it up. One of my favourite texts is in Hebrews 11, 'All these were still living by faith when they died.' Isn't that a marvellous text?

Having indicated who the letter is from and who it is addressed to, Jude gives the greeting: 'May you experience all you can hold of his mercy, peace and love.' [or, alternatively: 'I want you to be filled to your capacity . . . .'] This means to take every bit you can hold, not just have a *taste* of mercy, peace and love but have every bit you can take in, so that your life is full to overflowing with these three things. What a beautiful greeting. Do you notice that there is one word missing that Christians always used to use? 'Grace'. Why did he not include that? He replaces it with the word 'love'. Others write, 'Grace and mercy and peace', but he doesn't, because grace, he is going to show, is the word that has been twisted and misused in their fellowship, and he dare not use it until he has corrected them. It is tragic when you have to forgo the delight of using Christian words because they are so misunderstood, and this happens to biblical words. I went to speak to a youth club in a downtown urban area, and as I went in to the young people, the youth club leader said, "David, you can tell them about God but, whatever you do, don't use the word 'father' and don't use the word 'love'." Fancy being asked to talk about God and told you cannot use those two words! I made the mistake of using the word 'love', and a teenage girl sitting in the front row made an obscene gesture at me straight away.

Then I realised that these two beautiful words had been so abused. Most of them had never known someone called 'father', and never had any love, so I could not use the words. Jude cannot use the word 'grace' because it has been so misused, and we are going to see how.

Then Jude tells of why he is writing. When you write a letter you have to have something in common with the person to whom you are sending it. There is no point in writing unless there is something you both share. So his words mean: I am writing to you because you have got a problem and I am concerned about it. I was fully intending to write another kind of letter to you and then I found I had to write this one. There is a note of regret there.

Now I share his experience. When I was preparing to teach at a Christian event, I thought, 'Oh God, give me a lovely word that'll cheer everybody up and get us all blessed out of our boots — and please can I talk about the salvation we share?' But the Lord said, 'Preach on Jude,' and when I read Jude again, I thought, 'Oh, no!' But I had to, and I think it must be because the Lord knows more than I do about the situations of churches and Christians, and he wants this word given.

So what was the problem? Jude's message is: I'm concerned about you, you're in real danger, and the danger is due to the fact that people have sneaked into your fellowship and are spoiling it. They wormed their way in, they came in subtly; you didn't even notice the influence.

The tragedy is that people have not noticed what has happened to the church of Jesus Christ in this country, it has happened so gradually. We have hardly been aware of what happens outside the church. It is missionaries who come back after five years and go through London, who see what has really happened. It is rather like your hair: you don't really notice it is growing, do you? It is other people who notice it if they have not seen you for a while. They may notice how it is receding. But we do not notice these things that happen so gradually and so subtly. Something has been happening: there is a cancerous growth in the church in this land that has been coming on for over seventy years, and people have hardly noticed how it has crept in among us — and it is the same problem they had in the church to which Jude wrote. So instead of just sharing blessings with his readers (which is always lovely because writing a letter sharing a blessing with someone always multiplies it), Jude was saying: I am having to write to you to urge you: please keep up the fight for the true faith. The word he actually uses in the Greek means he is urging them to *agonise* for the true faith. Nobody said it was going to be easy. It is painful, costly, sacrificial to go on in the struggle for the true faith, and the true faith is the faith that was delivered to the saints at the beginning. The fact that people in the churches of this land have changed the gospel means we are losing the battle in the nation. We have watered it down, neutralised it, compromised it, and that is why we are so ineffective —because it is only the truth that sets people free. Men's opinions never set anyone free, and we think we have to change the gospel to meet modern needs!

I was at Cambridge as a student, and a man took me through Paul's letter to the Romans in such a way that I still owe a lot to him. He planted the gospel of Paul (which is the only gospel there is anyway) into my soul, by taking me through that epistle. He was a fine Bible student, a Cambridge professor. He had an uncle (J Armitage Robinson), who in the nineteenth century was one of the leading Bible scholars of this land, but it is unlikely that you have heard of him. You will have heard of the nephew, John Robinson. He took me through the Bible and taught me the word of God, and then they made him a bishop. He went to London as Bishop of Woolwich and found he had nothing to say. He could not communicate to the working men of east or south-east London. So he thought: I must change the gospel. He changed the gospel and put his new gospel in a book entitled *Honest To God*. Now you know who I am talking about! Suddenly it was a bestseller and he got it all from German theologians called Bultmann and Tillich, and one or two others, and he preached this brand new gospel. It sold like hot cakes in Japan to the Shintoists, because they said, 'This is our gospel.' At the same time, Richard Wurmbrand was in prison in Eastern Europe and the communists brought him a copy of *Honest to God* and said, 'Read that.' When he had read it, they said, 'If you will say that is your

Christianity, we'll set you free.' He replied, 'That is not my Christianity,' and he stayed in jail.

The man who taught me Paul's letter to the Romans, and later changed the gospel to try to fit it to the twentieth century, died some years ago, but before he died he had come back to the Bible, praise God! He returned to Cambridge, went back to the word of God and wrote *The Dating of the New Testament*, which is one of the best biblical books that has been written. Although he returned to his biblical faith, meanwhile the damage had been done. Thousands lost their faith because he changed the gospel.

I wonder if you realise just how widely this has happened and what a subtle effect it has had on all of us, and I am going to show you how. But this is what Jude was saying, this is his burden. His plea meant: 'Please, I urge you, continue the agonising struggle for the true faith which was once and for all delivered to the early saints.' We have that gospel delivered to the saints in our New Testament and I am so thrilled that it was not delivered to the theologians or the bishops, it was delivered to the *saints* — and that includes you! Every Christian is called of God to continue the painful struggle for the true faith that was once and for all delivered.

Incidentally, maintaining that struggle has nothing to do with education, for the truth is available to any man or woman who is childlike enough to believe it and to do it. The best theologians are those who do what God tells them to do. The truth has been entrusted to you, to pass on to your children and your grandchildren — and if we mess it up, what will happen to them?

Now how was it being messed up by these sneaky people who had wormed their way into a fellowship that they had not planted? There are some people who love to get hold of other's converts and change their ideas. They like to build on other men's foundations, and these people had just come in and were subtly making changes. There were just two things they were doing — they were devastating in their effect, and when I mention them you will realise how relevant Jude is to the century in which we have to contend for the true faith.

The first thing they were doing was twisting the grace of God into an excuse for immorality. Now the grace of God is the loveliest doctrine of all in the New Testament, and the word 'grace', to those who understand it, is the most beautiful word. It means that Christianity is totally different from every other religion in the world, because there is no other religion that has grace at the heart of it. What do I mean by that? Other religions teach: you clean your life up and you will be acceptable to God; start climbing the ladder of holiness, and at the top God will accept you. Or, to put it in simple terms, get sanctified and God will justify you. The only religion in the world that reverses that is our religion of grace, which says that no matter how bad you are, God will justify you — he is the friend of sinners; the

Father and the Son are friends of bad people.

I had the chance to preach on a major Canadian television channel and the producer said: 'You can speak about anything you like for twenty minutes. What do you want to talk about?'

'I'd love to speak about the kingdom of God,' I replied. They were a bit surprised, but anyway for twenty minutes I spoke about the kingdom of God, tried to tell people what it means. There were telephones in the studio for viewers to phone in, and the first telephone rang. A woman's voice said, 'I'm a hooker (that is Canadian for 'prostitute') on the streets of Toronto, and I want to ask one question, "How can I get into that kingdom?"' I thought: we are back to the New Testament — you preach the kingdom and the prostitutes want to get in. You can tell whether people are preaching the true gospel by what kind of people are responding to it, because the gospel of the kingdom is bad news to religious people, it is bad news to respectable people, and it is great news for sinners because the gospel of grace says God accepts you as you are, which is the most wonderful news that has ever been told. What good news!

But what does that mean? It means two things. I was invited to go and speak to a Baptist Women's League meeting. I feel like a lion in a den of Daniels in those situations. A big lady in a fur coat met me and said, 'Are you the speaker for this afternoon?' I said that I was.

'What are you going to speak on, because I'm the

chairperson'? When she heard that I meant to speak on grace she said, 'Oh, that sounds nice.'

So I got up and began my talk: 'I want to say just two things to you, two things which grace means. First, your bad deeds need not keep you out of heaven, because that is what grace means; and, second, your good deeds will not help you to get there.'

Well, they loved the first half! But the chairperson came up to me afterwards, shaking with upsetness, and said: 'Are you trying to tell me that all the good things I've ever done have been wasted?'

My reply was: 'As far as other people are concerned they were not wasted, they helped other people; as far as you're concerned they won't help you.'

She said, 'I thought that's what you were saying.' I never got invited back to that Baptist women's league!

Grace is offensive to good people because it means you have to repent of your good deeds. Most people think repentance is concerned with your bad deeds — and it is, but not entirely. Repentance involves leaving your good deeds behind, and saying: nothing in my hands I bring. Shall I tell you what good deeds are to God, how they feel to God? Well forgive me for being blunt but the more you read the Bible in the original language the more earthy it gets. Our English versions were translated for polite congregations! So let me tell you what it actually means. Isaiah says: your righteousness is like a menstrual cloth. Ladies will understand that language. That is not something you want to parade or boast about. Now one for the men: Paul, in Philippians chapter 3, said: When I consider my good deeds, the commandments I have kept [not the commandments he had broken, notice; he only broke one out of ten, and coveting was the one that he couldn't handle] —when I look at the nine I kept, I feel like a little boy who has emptied his bowels into a chamber pot and is holding it up and saying, look what I've done. The word he uses, which is translated 'dung' in the Authorised Version, is a crude Greek word for human excrement. It stinks! So grace says: you get rid of all your good deeds as well as your bad deeds. That is bad news for people who have done 'Meals on Wheels' for twenty years, or who have been in the Women's Institute or have been in Rotary, and such like. You would be amazed how many people in Britain are hoping they have done enough good deeds to the neighbour and grandmother and the cat to get to glory! Grace means *nothing* — no bad deeds — can keep you out; no good deeds can get you in. God says: I accept you as you are for the sake of my Son Jesus Christ. It is the only gospel there is. Now that is a beautiful gospel and we love to sing about it. Yet 'grace' is the most misunderstood word in England. Shall I tell you why? For the same reason as Jude is outlining here, it has been assumed that because God accepts you as you are, that it does not matter how you live after that; that God's grace is such that we can do anything we like really, and he will forgive. In other words, there is a sentimental view of God, and it is that sentimental view of God which is pervading even evangelical circles. How do I know this? Consider, in the past year, have you heard a sermon on hell in your fellowship? The fact is that we have twisted grace to mean that there is nothing to worry about, that God is not that kind of God, that he would not hurt a fly.

Some time ago on television, an agnostic lady interviewer was talking to a bishop who chaired a commission for revising doctrine in the Church of England. She asked him, 'Are you coming to a different view of God in your discussions?' He said that they had.

'Oh,' she said, 'what have you learned about God that is new?'

He replied, 'We are understanding that God is as weak as water.' To make sure viewers heard it, he repeated the expression: 'as weak as water'.

She said, 'What do you mean?'

'Well,' he said, 'this world is in a mess, isn't it? God is looking to us to get it out of the mess for him. He is relying on us to do it.'

She was staggered at this and asked, 'How do you imagine God?'

He replied, 'I like to think of a large family in which there is a grandmother, and her love keeps the whole family together while they go out and do the work.'

And the agnostic lady interviewer said to him, 'I thought God was a father, not a grandmother.'

My wife was angry (which is extremely rare!) and

she said: 'That's blasphemy.' It is —God as a harmless old granny in the corner! That is how most people think of God. They do not think he would ever hurt anyone; they do not fear him, because they do not think he could harm them, or that he would.

In 1984, York Minster went up in flames. An architect explained to me that a lightning conductor system had been installed to protect three million pounds' worth of recent renovation work, and that smoke detectors had been placed throughout the building. The entire lightning conductor system was blown, and every smoke detector was put out of action by a million volt strike of lightning that started the fire! The architect looked me in the face and said, 'That was God, wasn't it?' The fire chief who put it out was convinced it had been started by a divine arsonist. A meteorological map shows that there was no cloud over the whole of Yorkshire for that day, except for one little cloud that circled York Minster for twenty minutes and should have produced no more than a few drops of rain. But out of it came that million volt strike of lightning, with no thunder whatever. I heard of sixteen meteorologists, not one of them a believer, who said: 'That was God.'

Standing outside the smouldering ruins of York Minster the very next day, my back against the wall close to where David Watson had ministered, I trembled. The Archbishops said it not only was not God but it could not have been, because God would never do such a thing! Have they never heard of Sodom and

Gomorrah? It was Billy Graham who said that if God does nothing about England and America he will have to apologise to Sodom and Gomorrah. That was one of the few prophetic words I had heard from Billy, but it was straight from the Lord's heart. We have so come to a sentimental view of God, thinking that he's really a nice old person upstairs — and we get pally with him, assuming he wouldn't hurt a fly.

We have heard a great deal about signs and wonders, we have heard about the power of the Holy Spirit to make the blind see, and to raise the dead. But when did you hear, in all that talk of signs and wonders, that the same power of the Holy Spirit which can make the blind see can make the seeing blind? That is what Paul did in Cyprus.

I was walking through Cyprus by myself on the very road that Paul and Barnabas followed, and I read of how, when they confronted an occult magician, Paul said, 'In the name of Jesus be blind', the man lost his sight and the governor of Cyprus was converted! (See Acts 13:4-11.) When did you hear that preached about? And what about raising the dead? By the same power of the Holy Spirit the living can be killed. Somebody asked me at a ministers' seminar some time ago: 'Do you believe in being slain in the Spirit?' I said, 'Of course I do, it's biblical — Ananias and Sapphira were — if you want to be slain in the Spirit, then all you have to do is lie about what you put in the collection and have Simon Peter as your pastor!' That stopped the conversation quickly. When those two church members lied to the Holy Spirit, great fear came upon people both inside and outside the church, and people did not dare go near them. The fear of God began to touch people. We are a long, long way from that.

It is distorting the grace of God and you just do not understand grace if you think it means that because he has accepted you as you are, you can stay that way —that because he has forgiven your sins you can go on sinning. Imagine that you see a man drowning in a river. You pull your jacket and shoes off and dive in and pull him out, and then he shakes your hand and says, 'Oh brother, you've saved my life, thank you so much.' Then he turns round and walks back into the river, and shouts again, 'Help, save me, save me' —and you dive in again, you pull him out and get him dry. Then he says, 'Oh that's twice you've saved me, I'm just so grateful to you' — and he turns round and walks back in again! How many times are you going to pull him out? Do you know what you will be thinking if not saying before long? You will say: 'You don't want to be saved.' Grace does not mean that you can live the way you like for the rest of your life and God will forgive you. He only accepted you so that you could stop doing what you were doing. That is his amazing method: to reform us, not to let us off.

Years ago, I met a man who was the headmaster of a young offenders' institution, then known as a 'borstal'. There was a boy he could do nothing with. He gave him the soft treatment, privileges, but they were abused. They tried removing privileges, but still he did not respond. Nothing worked with that boy and it was clear what his future would be: in and out of prison. Every attempt to get him straightened out failed. One day my friend called that boy into his office and said: 'Now look, I have tried every way I know to help you to pull yourself up, and I have failed. There is only one other thing I can do, and I can't do it without your permission and I'm asking your permission to do it.'

The boy replied, 'What's that?'

My friend said, 'I want to adopt you as my son. I want you to come and live in my house. I want you to carry my surname. I can't do that unless you're willing. And if you get into trouble after that it is my name that will be dragged in the mud, but I'm prepared to face that. I'm only asking you to say yes, that's all.'

The boy was totally taken aback, but he finally muttered 'okay', and he went to live in the man's home as his son with his name. If I told you that from that day he lived a beautiful, good life I would be telling you a lie, but if I tell you that he began to, and that he wanted to from that day, I would be telling you the truth. Do you understand what I am saying? Grace is not God's way of saying you can live the way you want, you can do anything you like and I'll forgive you. That is an abuse of the grace of God — it makes the grace of God an excuse for immorality, which is what was happening in the church to which Jude wrote.

All of us, have taken the grace of God and abused it that way, because we thought, 'It's alright, there is no condemnation now for those who are in Christ Jesus, no fear of him doing anything to us now — it's okay. Yes, I'm sorry I did it but it's not too serious after all, I'm a child of God, I'm saved and once saved always saved.'

That is how we have talked to ourselves, and we shall fall into the trap of the German poet Heine whose last words when dying in Paris after a lifetime of sin were, 'God will forgive me, that's his business.' Now it may shock you to have it put in such blunt terms by Heine, but Hebrews chapter 10 talks about insulting the Spirit of grace by going on sinning after you have received grace. It is an insult to grace to go on the way you did after God has accepted you as you are. Yet the sentimental view of God does not believe God would destroy, does not believe God would judge, does not believe God would visit, does not believe God would let me get sick, does not believe God would do me any harm — so we do not want to know about judgment, about hell; we do not want to know about God's severity. Yet if you understand God well, you would say with the apostle, 'Behold then the goodness and the severity of God.' You get a magnified view of God when you see how this hangs together.

I came across an appalling account of a tragedy in the little island of Martinique. In 1902, the town of Saint-Pierre was obliterated by an exploding volcano. The mountain began to rumble and the people were not too bothered (it had rumbled before), but this time Mont Pelée erupted and the lava flowed over the town, wiping out everybody in the direct path (around 30,000 people) except for two survivors, one of whom was in jail. Because he was in an underground cell he escaped. I read of that tragic event and thought of how terrible it was. Later I heard the rest of the story. A few days before the eruption happened there was a religious festival and a holiday, but in Martinique religious festivals had become a carnival and were orgies, fun days rather than holy days, and on that fun day, a few days previously they had put on a mock religious procession through Saint-Pierre. They had carried a big wooden cross and they had nailed a pig to the cross and labelled it 'holy Jesus' and walked through that town holding that pig on a cross called 'holy Jesus'. The editor of the local newspaper joined in the 'fun' and said, 'I dare God to show us he's still alive.' Three days later the entire city had gone. God is not to be trifled with. We abuse the grace of God if we think it means you can live how you like and God will forgive, all he wants you to be is happy.

There is a very subtle form of this abuse of God's grace that has crept in without being noticed. It started in the middle of the 1980s (which came to be called the 'me' decade) with a teaching in the name of Jesus that you have a duty to love yourself. Books came out under that title. Jesus gave us two great commandments: Love the Lord your God with all your heart and soul and strength, and love your neighbour as yourself. Some clever people said, 'Ah, ". . . as yourself", that means it's alright to love yourself' — and they made it into three commandments: Love God, love your neighbour, love yourself! That was how this started.

It moved from loving yourself to expressing yourself: find out your gift, not with the purpose of helping others, but so that *you* can be fulfilled and satisfied. It moved on from there to, 'Enjoy yourself, God wants you to.' That went on inexorably to, 'Indulge yourself' — which means: do whatever you want to, God wants you to. It started with something that seemed right but gradually changed. So overweight Christians were not worried: 'It's alright, I enjoy my food, yes I'm a bit overweight . . . .' They forgot that the body is the temple of the Holy Spirit. 'Oh, but God wants me to enjoy my food.' Yes, that is true, but not *that* true.

One of our appetites, when we get to the stage of 'indulging yourself', will be in the sexual area, because that is one of our strongest appetites, and standards in that area have gone down and down, inside church as well as outside. That was what had happened in the church to which Jude wrote. You know it is true! The grace of God was never intended to lead to anything of self, Jesus never said 'Love yourself'; he never said, 'Express yourself', 'Enjoy yourself'; 'Indulge yourself'. The only thing he said about yourself was: deny yourself and come with me. The self-centeredness of the outside world has got in even among us, so that we have become almost preoccupied with our own problems, our own self-expression, finding *my* place in the body of Christ; finding *me, me, me, me*.

I once met a missionary who regularly went alone down a bandit infested road in Ethiopia and risked her life to go and preach the gospel, and I said to her, 'Aren't you afraid to die? Aren't you afraid of the danger down that road?' I will never forget her answer: 'I died ten years ago, so I can't die again'. Somebody else said to me about that missionary, 'I would never call her unselfish, I would call her self*less*.' Jude's message is: these people who have come in among you are twisting the grace of God into an excuse for doing anything they want. That was not the grace of God, that is a travesty of grace; grace is not for that at all, your forgiveness is not for that.

This is reflected in so many hymns. 'He died that we might be forgiven,' says the hymn *There is a Green Hill Far Away*. But do not stop there, the next line gets it right: 'He died to make us good.' That is grace. It may be free to you but it cost everything to Jesus, and if you realise that, grace can only come to you. God can only accept you as you are because Jesus paid for it with his life, and you must never take that lightly. That is why Christians are exhorted to take bread and wine regularly, so that they never forget the cost. It may be cheap to you but it was very, very expensive to Jesus; that is why it is on offer — it is free.

The other way in which some were perverting the

true faith was they were denying Jesus Christ as their only Master and Lord. Now I want to affirm something of which you may not yet be fully aware, but you must be if you are going to fight for the true faith in this country. Notice that it is the grace of God and the person of Christ that they have twisted. So they are not 'unchristian'; they believe in God and in his grace, they believe in Jesus Christ: you would take them for full Christians — that is how they get right in and sneak into the fellowship. They use the term 'the grace of God', they talk about Jesus Christ, and therefore you have to be doubly aware of what they mean when they say this.

The real danger does not come from atheists. There are not too many real atheists around and they are not a danger to the church. Agnostics are not even the main danger to the church. The main danger to the church is people within the church who use the right language with the wrong meaning. That is where the battle is being fought. Here is something I want to say to you as clearly as I can, so that you grasp it. Do not be fooled by people who say they believe in Jesus, because 'religion' is not on the way out. Man is basically religious and always will be, and although Christianity is declining in Britain and has been since World War I, that does not mean religion is in decline. Religion is always part of man's make up, and if he turns away from one religion he will turn towards another. The communists found that you cannot kill religion in man. Some religions are growing in England. Occultism is growing, and that is a religion; Islam is growing in England, too. So do not think that religion is on the way out, it is not, but religion has changed.

The complicating factor is this: in my early days England was Christian — most people knew what church they were staying away from, and 98% of the population were buried by a Christian clergyman. Three-quarters of the people in England were married in a Christian church. And in the late twentieth century two-thirds of the people in England had been christened as babies in a Christian church. (It doesn't seem to have 'taken' but they were!) At a time when the Church of England alone had baptised 27 million of the population of England (about half) only around 700,000 of them had stayed, which is an appalling wastage. But Britain was 'Christian', and other religions were so far away that we did not think missionary work began this side of the Mediterranean. Nobody thought of Europe as a missionary field then.

What has happened? Over recent decades, with the immigration of so many people, suddenly here in England we are surrounded by other religions. Many mosques are being built, while many chapels and churches have closed. Religion is shifting. When I was a boy, in Newcastle upon Tyne there were seven churches within about a quarter of a mile of my home, and there is only one of those left now. But on 25th December some years ago, a Satanist 'church' was opened in my home town, near my boyhood home. Now here is the subtlety: how are we going to cope with the fact that England is no longer a 'one religion' country, it is now a 'many religions' country? Birmingham now has the muezzin crying morning prayers from the minaret of the mosque over loudspeakers where once there were only church bells, and the Christians are upset about it. Why should they be? They have had the privilege of church bells for so long. On what conceivable ground can we deny freedom to the Muslims? It is pure tradition that says this is a Christian country. It is not a Christian country — only two to three percent of the population of this nation are convinced Christians.

Do you know how the 'man in the street' has decided to live with this fact of England being a 'multi-religion' country? He has decided that all religions are right. That is how he is managing to live with his neighbour. He is saying: 'It's alright if you're a sincere Muslim; it's alright if you're a sincere Hindu, we're all seeking the same God.' That is how we are coping with what is called a pluralist society, and it is in our schools. Where once the Bible was taught in Religious Knowledge, now it is Comparative Religion.

The more you are confronted with other religions, the more difficult it is to say, 'You are wrong'. So people now are accepting that everybody is right, all shall win and all shall have prizes; we must learn to live with each other.

The key word in Jude v. 4 is 'only'. You see, people are very favourable towards Jesus. Islam accepts Jesus,

Buddhism accepts Jesus, many occult religions accept Jesus. Jesus is popular, Jesus is news, even some Jews now accept Jesus, but not many of them accept him as the 'only'. In all these other religions he is one among others, and people are perfectly happy for you to believe in Jesus as long as you are willing to say he is only one among the others, only a prophet, only a 'superstar'. But he is not just a prophet, he is not a superstar, he is the only Master and Lord, he is the only way to God, and none of the other religions will get you to God. Jesus is the *only* name whereby we can be saved, and that is going to cut you off from a whole lot of people who are willing to accept Jesus as one among others. A lot of Christians are being fooled by people because they say, 'Oh yes, I believe in Jesus', but, if you press them, they do not believe he is the only one. Ask, 'Do you believe he is the *only* way, not just *a* way; the *only* truth, not just *a* truth; the *only* life, not just *a* life?' —and you will find they do not. They are willing to accept him as one great man among others. Be aware— that view is right inside the churches. Did you know that? The view that Jesus was one of the greatest men who ever lived, and a man who got nearer to God than perhaps any other man — this has been preached in my own denomination (Baptist), by the principal of a theological college. A few of us got up and said, 'That is not the truth.' I think that finished my career in the denomination —because that was not saying Jesus is the *only*.

Now that is the dividing line —between those who

say Jesus is one among others, perhaps the greatest, and those who say, 'No, he is the only Master and Lord.' Just as a sentimental view of the grace of God has crept in, so a syncretistic view of the person of Jesus has crept in, which puts him alongside others.

There is a big round building in the middle of Rome, still there though it is two thousand years old. It is a magnificent circular temple and inside are alcoves all the way around. There is a big hole in the middle of the ceiling that lets the sun in. It is called the Pantheon, meaning 'all gods'. As soon as the Romans conquered a nation, they said: we will put your god in among all ours so that we can have one religion for the whole empire. So when they conquered Greeks, the Greek gods were put in alcoves in the Pantheon. They offered the Jews a place for an image of Jehovah, and the Jews said no. Jesus would never be erected there. I take great delight in telling you that now if you go to the Pantheon every one of those alcoves is empty because it is now a Christian church — for Jesus only. Go and look at it. He is not one among many, he is the only Son of God, the only Saviour. If we allow our thinking to accept syncretism — to accept that other religions are valid — then I will tell you what will happen: missionary work will be killed off, and missionary work has been seriously in decline in this country. Why? Because the vague idea, even among evangelical Christians, is: well, why do we really need to go and evangelise? Their religion is good enough for them, they are sincere, so why do we need to upset their culture? Have you heard this kind of talk? It is being broadcast on your television again and again. That was what was happening in the church to which Jude wrote. They were watering down the grace of God and making it an excuse for living any old how. They were watering down the theology of Jesus, and teaching: he is not the only one you need to listen to; he is a good one, he is a great one, but he is not the only one.

Those are the two great issues of the faith for which we are fighting today, painfully struggling for the true faith once delivered to all the saints — a grace of God that says to you: I have given you my grace so that you can live right. The prostitute on the streets of Toronto told us why she had asked the question, 'How can I get into that kingdom?' She said, '... because I want to live right.' That is the only point of receiving the grace of God because that is what it is for — and you will only do it and receive that grace to live right when you say, 'Jesus is the only Master and the only Lord in my life, there is no one beside him.'

We will look at how this works out in our conduct, our character, and our conversation. If we once start losing the true faith we will learn from that negatively. Then we will conclude our study very positively on what to do about the whole situation, and how we can fight the good fight. Are you ready for a fight? A fight inside the church, not outside?

A schoolteacher whose subject was Religious

Knowledge once said to his class, 'Who knocked down the walls of Jericho?' There was silence. The teacher said, 'Come on, come on, I want to know, who knocked down the walls of Jericho?' Finally, a little boy with spectacles called Smith put up his hand and said, 'Please sir, I didn't.' So later, in the staffroom, the teacher met the headmaster and said, 'Headmaster, a funny thing happened in my Religious Knowledge lesson today. I asked the class who knocked down the walls of Jericho and young Smith said, "Please sir, I didn't."' And the headmaster said, 'Well I know Smith and I know his family, and if he said he didn't I'm sure he didn't.' So the teacher explained a bit and the headmaster then thought it was quite funny. So later on, when the Inspector of Education arrived in the school, the headmaster thought he would tell him. He said, 'Inspector, quite a funny thing happened in our Religious Studies class this morning. The teacher said "Who knocked down the walls of Jericho", and a young boy called Smith said, "Please sir, I didn't."' The Inspector thought a bit, and then he said, 'Well, it's probably too late to find out who did it. You had better get it repaired and send the bill in.'

That is a neat way of saying that ignorance about the word of God in our nation is appalling. And whose fault is it? Ours. I have little sympathy with Christians who are praying that God will raise up a prophet to point a finger at the nation of England and tell it how wicked it is. What I hear is that God's prophetic word is being directed to the people really responsible for the state of the nation — and the people who are responsible are the people inside the church. The state of the nation is only a reflection of the state of the church. It is our responsibility. If we had been what God wanted us to be in the church, the nation would not be as it is today. If there is ignorance out there of the word of God it is because we knew it and have not told them. That is my burden. Therefore the Lord is speaking more to the church in England than the nation of England, as I hear him, because it is hypocrisy to go and tell the nation to put its house in order when we were not prepared to put the church in order and have the Holy Spirit reform us.

I find that most people in the church want revival but not reformation. They want a bit more life in the services, a few more guitars and a bit of good chorus singing and a lot of aerobic worship. But when I speak about what the Spirit wants to change in the church, that is a different story. They want him to renew what is already there, but not change it.

I tell you this very solemnly, this is not a direct word of the Lord from me, I heard it at the mouth of a young Baptist pastor. I was at a meeting of three hundred Baptist pastors and they said they were going to have an evening praying for a revival, and we started. We said: 'Lord, revive the Baptists; revive the denomination; revive the Baptist Union', and so on. The prayers got no higher than the ceiling, you could feel it. Then the young Baptist pastor got up and said: 'Thus says the

Lord, "I will not revive what I never built."' And shivers went down my spine. You know when you hear a word of prophecy, it is not just a nice little 'Bless you my children, I love you', it is a word that goes to the root of the problem, a word that lays bare and a word that reveals the secrets of your heart. We are asking him to revive what we have got, and he never built most of what we have got. He is wanting to reform us, not just renew us, and to restore his image in us.

I hope that you are now beginning to get to feel you know Jude and understand something of what he is saying. One of the advantages of reading the Bible straight through is that you have to read the bits you do not like. You cannot pick and choose, and a preacher cannot duck the difficult passages. In the next section we are going through a bit of a dark valley, a kind of smoky glass mirror in which we might see things that we did not want to see. And we need to hear the whole word of God.

2

LEARNING FROM THE PAST
Read 5–19

This section is built on the assumption that the God of the Old Testament is the God of the New Testament as well. You would be amazed how many people do not believe that. The first famous man in church history who denied it was called Marcion, and from him we got the Marcionite heresy. Marcion was the first man to say I don't like the God of the Old Testament, I will only have the God of the New Testament, as if they were two different Gods. He thought that the 'God of the Old Testament' seems to be a God who punishes, but the 'God of the New Testament' seems to be a God who wants to let us off. The 'God of the Old Testament' sends people to war and slaughters them, but the 'God of the New Testament' is a pacifist. Marcion wanted a God like that, so he decided to cut the Old Testament out of his Bible. But it was not long before he found he had to start cutting bits out of the New Testament as well, because it says some of the same things. The statement 'our God is a consuming fire', is not only in Deuteronomy, it is in the letter to the Hebrews. And he had to start cutting out the Book of Revelation because there was a God of war again and a Christ who rode, not on a donkey of peace, but on a white horse of war, and made war against the united nations, and left the dead for the birds to pick. That is a different Jesus, isn't it? No, it is not! It is the same Jesus, the Jesus who came in great tenderness and mercy the first time around is coming back, but he will come back for a very different reason. He has been already to do everything he can to save people, so he is coming the next time to deal with those who refuse to be saved. It is the same Jesus and it is the same God, so Jude says don't forget the God of the Old Testament. If you do, you will likely get a distorted view.

You see, the Old Testament was the Bible that Jesus was brought up on, the Bible he believed in — every word — and the God of the Old Testament is the God and Father of our Lord Jesus. He is the Jewish God, the God of Abraham, Isaac and Jacob; he is the God of Elijah, he is the God of Moses, and he is the God of Jesus. He is the same God all the way through. And if only people would not forget what kind of a God he is, there would be more fear of God in Britain. According to an opinion poll, 67% of the British people believe in God. Well, bully for them! It doesn't mean a thing. The question that is important to ask is not 'Do you believe in God or do you not?', it is 'What kind of a God do you believe in?' I would like an opinion poll to ask people: 'Do you fear God?' And I would guess that no more than 2% of the population are afraid of God. He is portrayed on television and radio as a nice old boy who just wants to pat you on the head and say, 'Oh, we'll forgive and forget, all I want you to be is happy.' Nothing could be further from the truth. Kenneth Taylor puts the fourth verse of Jude like this: *These men are saying that now you have become a Christian you can do anything you like without any fear of God's punishment.* That is the false teaching that distorts the grace of God.

Here is something that will shock you, but we need to hear it: Christians need to fear God's punishment. I have said before that because you are being saved that does not mean you are safe. There are dangers for Christians that we need to be told about, and the letter of Jude is about them. But we do not want to hear that, we thought we had finished with God's punishment. Did you know that Christians are far more likely to be punished by God in this world than non-Christians? The Bible actually says that. God loves you too much to let you off. It is foolish to think that love never punishes. That is a sentimental view of love that too many parents today have. 'Spare the rod and spoil the child' is not old-fashioned, it is biblical truth. Behind that debate about corporal punishment lies a much larger one. Our generation does not want any punishment for anything. The whole debate about capital punishment was whether it deterred people from murdering. No it

71

does not deter anyone, people will still murder whether there is capital punishment or not. And there is no point in debating whether capital punishment reforms a character because once you have hanged him you can hardly reform him. The only reason for it was a very, very simple one and it is the principle of retribution, not deterrence, not reformation. In other words, a man who has robbed another of life deserves to lose his own. When Britain abolished capital punishment, my fear (and I expressed it at the time) was that the very next legislation would be on abortion, allowing us to kill our own babies. Why did I say that? Because the reason for abolishing capital punishment was that we had lost sight of the sacredness of human life, and murder is now treated as theft, whereas in God's sight it is sacrilege. You are touching the image of God when you take a life. You do not do that when you steal someone's property. As soon as the sacredness of life is lost, not only is capital punishment abolished, the next thing is you are allowed to kill off old granny and put her down like the dog. This is what happened in Nazi Germany in the 1930s and it could happen in Britain.

It is because people do not fear God any more that they do not respect his image in each other. A human life is just a human life now. It is not seen as the image of God because we no longer fear God. And God watches everything that goes on. Have you ever considered this: God has had to watch every rape? There has been a spate of young men breaking into pensioners' homes and raping women in their eighties and nineties. And God watches it. People think they have got away with it because nobody saw it. But one person saw it. Do you know what the definition of 'godlessness' is in the Bible? Godlessness is behaving as if God cannot see. That is all. Jude is saying these men who have got into your church are godless men. They talk about the grace of God, they talk about Jesus Christ, but they are godless. 'Godless' does not mean atheism, godlessness in the Bible is the lack of the fear of God. So Judas is saying that godlessness has got right inside the church and there is no fear of God —and the fear of God is related primarily to the possibility that God could punish you for what you have done. If you no longer believe in a God who punishes, you will not have any fear of God in you. That is what it is related to.

Why did I say you are more likely to be punished if you are a Christian? You are more likely to be punished in this world if you are a believer; you are more likely to be punished in the next world if you are a non-believer. So what you have done in becoming a believer is transferred the future punishment into the present. Because the epistle to the Hebrews says that if God does not chastise you when you go wrong you are a bastard, you are not his son. A father who loves a son punishes that son, but the difference between the punishment that God gives believers in this world and the punishment he gives unbelievers in the next world is that the punishment of believers in this world is for their reformation, whereas the punishment for the unbeliever in the next is for retribution. Punishment with hope is good. As Hebrews says, it is painful at the time but later you will be thankful that your parent spanked you. You will be grateful that you were loved enough. I am grateful to the friends I have who love me enough to tell me when I am doing wrong. They are your only real friends.

'Let love be genuine', says Paul. What is genuine love? Genuine love hates what is evil and loves what is good. It has to be both. If your parents never punished you, they did not love you with the love that God has for you. If you have the idea 'now I'm saved, God would never punish me', you had better think again. A reader with a healthy fear of God who reads Jude carefully discovers that a Christian is not safe from God's punishment. Even those who had been brought out of Egypt under the blood of the lamb and passed through the Red Sea thought they were safe. But God dealt with them. Even the very angels of God in heaven thought they were safe, and he dealt with them too. A healthy fear of God wants to get things put right quickly. That is the message.

So Jude goes right back to the first five books of the Bible. It might be an indication that he is writing to believers who were Jews. It goes right back to what we call the Pentateuch, the five books of Moses, on which every Jew based his whole religion. To the Jews, that was the most important part of the Old Testament. They read right through them every year, and they reach the last verse on the last day of the Feast of Tabernacles, then they praise God and celebrate that they can start Genesis 1:1 the next day. They will start all over again and go through the first five books. I suggest you could do that as well because the God of the first five books of the Bible is the God we praise and worship. He has not changed one little bit. He has not changed in how he deals with his people. The God who dealt with them will deal with us. The God who dealt with the people in the days of Noah is going to deal with England in the same way. Jesus said it: 'as it was in the days of Noah so it will be.' God is going to do it again at the end of history.

There are people today, even inside the church, who do not believe that the flood happened. Then they do not believe in Jesus, because Jesus believed it happened. Furthermore, Jesus actually preached to the people who were drowned in the days of Noah. So how can it be a myth? Jesus did not preach to myths, he preached to real people.

Jude is very fond of threes. I was told that a good preacher always has three points. If so, there are at least ten sermons in the Book of Jude because he keeps telling you three things. You are called, loved, kept — there is the first sermon. Second sermon: may you be filled with mercy, peace and love. Here is his next threesome. He said: I am going to remind you of three things that God once did and you know them perfectly well. I am just reminding you about them.

The real problem is you forget what you want to forget. Did you know that you actually never forget anything? Do you believe that? There are two signs of old age and I am getting there fast. One sign is a bad memory. But actually I have never forgotten a thing, I just have problems remembering it, but it is there, stored. Have you ever noticed how this applies to smells? A smell of lavender always reminds me of my grandmother. Suddenly I can recall a whole lot of memories about my grandmother when I smell lavender —things I thought I had forgotten. Have you had that kind of experience?

We had breakfast with an Australian who was going round the area, looking at the places he had brought his wife to before she died, and we had an interesting chat. He was a real tough man and his language was pretty colourful. His last word to me was, 'I'm seventy-four, and if God had wanted me to be a Christian before this he'd have done so.' I said, 'The choice was yours.'

'Neat answer,' he replied. He was picking up the memories, and I am quite sure that as he went around the places he had taken his wife, he would in a way recall some things, but he had difficulty bringing them to his conscious mind. Everything you have ever said is stored in your memory; everything you ever did is stored in your memory. Everything you ever felt is stored in your memory.

The trouble is that the things we do not want to

remember, we suppress — we put them in a drawer in our subconscious and lock the drawer, and that is where many of the things you are dealing with come from. People remember hurts and resentments and they go deep down. They do not realise that they are still there and have never been dealt with and pulled out of the drawer and thrown away. That is what causes so many Christians to be paralysed. The secret of living the Christian life is to remember. Remembrance is part of your salvation. That is why the Jews still celebrate the Passover every year, so that they may remember the God who brought them out of Egypt. Remember! If you forget things, you will go wrong. So Jude is reminding his readers of some of the truths they had already heard. Do not forget them or you will forget that God can punish. And, he says: God brought two and a half million people out of Egypt and then he slaughtered them all, except two. You need to remember that. They thought they were safe, but even after having been brought out of Egypt with a mighty hand . . . . And what a miracle that was!

I heard of a liberal preacher (do you know what that is? —a preacher who reads the Bible with a pair of scissors in his hand, and he cuts out all the miracles) and he was preaching on the exodus. He said there was not a miracle at the exodus because the Red Sea was only eighteen inches deep at that place and at that time of the year, and the Hebrews just waded across. A lady in the congregation shouted 'Hallelujah!'

'Why did you shout "Hallelujah"?' he said.

'The great miracle,' she replied.

'What great miracle?'

'Drowning the Egyptian army in eighteen inches of water,' she said. Whichever way you look at it, it was a mighty miracle. But there were mightier miracles than the parting of the Red Sea. Their shoes never wore out in forty years. I have climbed Mount Sinai; I went up at three o'clock in the morning before the sun was up and before it got too hot. At the very top I found a little Jewish girl reading the Ten Commandments in Hebrew. I said to her, 'What is your name?'

'Miriam,' she replied.

I said, 'My, you've been around a long time.' But the point is I had a pair of sandals and they broke because of the stony desert floor and climbing Mount Sinai. My sandals would not take two days of it, yet the sandals of the Hebrews did not wear out in forty years. What a miracle! To me that seems an even bigger one than crossing the Red Sea.

And they got enough fresh water in a triangular desert, the Sinai, a peninsula in which the Egyptian army in 1973 was dying within three days because they had no food or water. But in that same place God gave fresh water for two and a half million people, to say nothing of the animals. He gave them food every day, delivered bread from heaven, and he did that every day for forty years. You work out the amount of bread that was needed for two and a half million people for forty years and you will get some idea of the mighty power of God — and you would have thought: they will trust him now forever. If I had been brought through the Red Sea and my shoes never wore out and I had all this bread and fresh water appearing miraculously in the desert, wouldn't I trust God? But he destroyed them all because they would not trust him.

The point actually came very much earlier than when the forty years were up — after only eleven days in Sinai. It only takes that long to get from Sinai into the promised land, yet it took them 14,549 days to do the journey. Why? Because they would not trust him. They reached the very edge of the promised land and then they got cold feet. They got to Kadesh, they could see into the land flowing with milk and honey, and they decided to do something they should never have done: to send spies in. They said to Moses, 'Let's send people in to find out what we are going to be up against.' To know the future can be fatal. If God had revealed to me what troubles I would get into in doing what I am doing now, I would never have done it. But a merciful God does not tell you what you are heading for, and we ought not to find out. We should just trust him and go forward.

They sent the spies in — twelve of them, one from each tribe — and ten of them saw giants and two of them saw grapes. They came back and two of them said: 'We've seen grapes, look at them, we've brought some for you.' The other ten said, 'We saw giants.' The

Hebrews were little people and the Canaanites were big people, and they lived in towns with walls that seemed to touch the clouds. The ten spies said 'We'll never make it', and God was angry. He said, 'Have I not carried you, as a father carries a son, all the way from Egypt?' Now how does a father carry a son? —up on his shoulders! I can remember having been carried by my father like that when I was just four years old — and I was the giant, because I could look over a six foot high garden fence! Although God had carried his people as a father carries a son, now they would not trust him so he told them that only the two who saw the grapes (Joshua and Caleb) would get into what he had promised. The fact that this is used by Jude (and by Paul) as an example to Christians means that Christians could fail to make it. Otherwise there is no point in drawing the parallel. A healthy fear of God says: I am going to go on believing, right to the end. The concept of faith in scripture is not one step that gets you there, it is a life of faith that gets you there. I dare to say that it is the faith you finish with that gets you into heaven, not the faith you start with. Because the verb 'believe' in the Greek New Testament is in what is called the present continuous tense, which is a particular Greek form of verb that means to *go on doing something* —not to do it once but to go on doing it. For example, Jesus used that tense when he said, 'Ask and you shall receive, seek and you will find, knock and it will be open to you.' If we are to translate that properly, we have: 'Go on asking and you will receive' — meaning not once, but go on until you get it. *Go on seeking* and you will find. *Go on knocking* and the door will open. Now listen to a verse that may be your favourite verse, but listen to it as it should be translated: *God so loved the world that he gave his only begotten Son, that whoever goes on believing in him will not perish but will go on having eternal life.* Does that sound a bit different to you now? It should do. Faith is *keeping faith*. 'Faith' and 'faithfulness' are the same word in Hebrew and Greek, and you never know whether to translate it faith or faithfulness because faith *goes on believing*.

The only reason God destroyed those Jews before they got to the promised land was not that they had been having immoral orgies, though they had. It was not because they had got into idolatry with calves, though they had. He destroyed them only for one reason: that they would not trust him after all he had done for them. That is the same God we deal with now. It is no use you saying: 'Twenty years ago I believed in him.'

Consider this question: when did you last believe in Jesus? Would you say, 'I've always done so'? No, you haven't! You might have to cast your mind back quite a long way to think of a situation in which you trusted him. If so, you are living on your past faith. John Wesley said: never do that . . . you are not safe that way. When Paul wanted to feel his security in the Lord, he didn't say: Well, my security rests in the fact that on the Damascus road many years ago I believed in Jesus. No, he said: The life I now live, I live by faith. That was his security. Have you noticed how often Paul in his letters, when he talks about our security, adds: *if you continue in the faith*. There it is. I do not believe in the 'perseverance of the saints', I believe in the word of God! There are two sides of 'keeping' — he is able to keep, and I have kept the faith. Jude begins by saying you are kept for Jesus Christ, and he ends by saying keep yourselves in the love of God. There are two sides to most questions in the Bible, and you can be sure that he will keep you because you are keeping on trusting him to keep you. That is the teaching of scripture, and God is angry when he has done so much for people — he has done so many miracles in their lives — if they come to a point where they say: 'I don't trust you, Lord'. After all he has done for us! Because he did a second exodus for us, too; and we have been under the blood of the Passover lamb as well; and we have got out of Egypt, and Satan's power over us has been broken. It is an absolute insult to say: 'God, I don't trust you now' — and that is what he is really concerned about. Are you trusting him *now*? Do you believe in him now like you used to?

That is what really matters — to *go on* believing until, like all the heroes of faith in Hebrews 11, it can be said of you what is said of them: '. . . and all these were still living by faith when they died', which is all the more remarkable because they did not see the results of their faith before they died. Abraham still believed in a city whose builder and maker was God, and he never saw it. They were living for something they never saw because God had something better — which was that Abraham is waiting for David Pawson to come along to enter into what he was believing for! That is what my Bible tells me: he is waiting for us; that Isaac and Jacob and Moses and Elijah are all waiting until we get there so that they can see the fruit of their faith. Isn't that beautiful? They died before they saw it, but they were still believing, still trusting, they never wavered. They went on believing, but the entire nation of Israel, except for two, did not go on believing and God punished them for it. One act of not trusting was enough for God to do that. We need to have a fear of God here to go on trusting him until we see him face to face.

The second example from the first five books of the Bible is an extraordinary story. It is about angels who had sex with human beings. The story is found in Genesis chapter 6 and one would rather not talk about it but I have to, it is in the word of God and we need to read it. Jude felt we needed to remember this extraordinary incident.

The angels are above us in the order of creation and there are thousands of them out there. Angels surround us. For all I know there may be some nearby now. I always used to think they might be 'up there' somewhere and they could be, or they could be sitting down in the room where you are sitting. Very often when angels appear, they look just like human beings. If angels had big wings and big harps and long white nighties all the time, can you imagine anyone entertaining an angel unawares? Which means very simply that you could have met one today and not have known it. Somebody sitting near you could be an angel. I am saying that to encourage you.

When I was in Dunedin, New Zealand some years ago, I met a man called Wayne. He was a plumber, about thirty years of age, and I met him just three weeks after he became a Christian. He had been converted and filled with the Spirit on the same day. He said, 'David, do you know, that night I went to bed and I fell asleep and I woke up at three in the morning, and there was an angel standing at the foot of my bed. And I was rather rude to him because I'd never spoken to an angel before and I didn't know how to speak.' I tried to look as if I did! But anyway I asked what he had said to the angel.

'Well,' he said, 'he just looked at me and pointed at me and said, "Wayne, today is your special day."'

Wayne had replied: 'You got your watch wrong mate, it's three in the morning. Yesterday was my special day.'

Then the angel said, 'Wayne, you're not listening, today is your special day.'

He said, 'Why, what's going to happen today? Is my wife going to get converted?' (She was still asleep, next to him.)

The angel replied, 'You're not listening Wayne, today is *your* special day.'

Wayne continued, 'You know, David, I finally got the

message: he was telling me not to live on the experience of yesterday. So now when I get up and shave, I look in the mirror and say, "Wayne, today is your special day." And in just three weeks I have had twenty-one special days.'

I could tell you many stories of how the angels have guarded people. One missionary on the Afghan border cycled down a road because he had to, knowing that there were bandits waiting at every corner to kill people. He arrived perfectly safely at his destination. Later, in the prison he met one of the bandits, who said, 'We nearly killed you, the day you rode your bike past our place.'

The missionary replied, 'Why didn't you kill me?'

'Oh,' he said, 'we would have, if it hadn't been for all the others on bicycles all round you.'

'How many were there?'

'Fifteen!'

So angels rode chariots in Bible days and they ride bicycles today. I could provide other examples.

The ministry of angels is beautiful, but some of them did something terribly wrong. We know how many of them did it — two hundred deserted their post, and they were the angels guarding Israel, under Michael. God has placed angels to guard the human race, and indeed the Bible indicates that one particular angel prince is set over each nation to look after it and to guard it, and the angel put over the nation of Israel to guard Israel was Michael. They came down to earth in the Mount

Hermon area, they saw women and wanted sex with them. Among themselves angels neither marry nor are given in marriage, but they can both desire sex and have it with human beings.

This could be related to Paul's remarks about how women dress in church. If you dress wrongly you are not only going to cause men to be tempted, you are going to cause angels to be tempted, and when Paul talked about head covering he said 'because of the angels'. Paul was advising women to say: I'm already taken, I already belong to someone else. In Genesis 6 we learn that those angels saw the women, and God had forbidden them to have sex with them, but they left their guarding duty and instead of guarding those human beings they seduced them. The result was hybrids living on earth, 'nephilim', monsters with superhuman strength. All kinds of horrible things resulted from this unnatural breeding. That was one of the main reasons God said that he regretted he ever made the human race. I believe that is the saddest verse in the Bible. I have heard parents say that in a courtroom of their own child: we wish we had never had him. God never said that about the trees and the mountains or the sea, he said it about us.

So what had people been doing? Two things. First of all, there was *independence* and second *indulgence*, and the Lord showed me that those two spirits often go together in someone's life; that a spirit of rebellion against authority, of refusal to be told, opens the way to a spirit of lust as well. The two can get into the human race — a spirit of insubordination, 'Nobody's going to tell me what to do', and a spirit of self-indulgence follows. We are dealing with very deep things now, and certainly the Lord can liberate us from all that. We will come back to that later. Now we are having to face facts. Those things went on just before the flood, and the angels were involved. The two hundred angels, because they deserted their post, would now be called demons, for demons are nothing more than angels who have deserted their post and are no longer under the control of the King of heaven. They do all kinds of damage and they are far more than a match for us. They are more intelligent, they are stronger than we are. But those particular ones will never do any further damage in this world because God took them and locked them in the lowest, darkest dungeon and he is going to keep them there until judgment day.

But Paul says don't tempt any others to do it, you women, especially in the presence of God in church. Because there is no salvation for the angels, there is no way they can ever be forgiven, no way they can ever be saved. Jesus did not die for the angels; not a single angel will ever be born again, not a single angel will ever be forgiven. Having seen the glory of God, having lived in heaven, once an angel sins and falls there is no hope for them, just that eternal punishment which the Lord has prepared for the devil and all his angels. Hebrews says that Jesus never died for the angels, the blood of Jesus is of no effect for the angels, but the blood of Jesus can help human beings. Isn't that an amazing thought? That is why, between Jesus' death and resurrection, he went and preached to those who had been drowned in the days of Noah. Did you ever wonder about that little titbit of information in Peter's letter? I think it must have come out when Peter met the risen Jesus in an encounter which is not recorded in scripture, so we do not know when or where, or what happened between them. Peter did not tell us. I would love to know what happened when Peter first met the risen Jesus by himself. I can imagine Peter saying: Jesus, where on earth have you been? — and Jesus might have said: I've not been on earth, but I've been preaching to the people who were drowned in Noah's day. There was hope even for the people who drowned in that day but not for the angels who did it.

That Jesus preached to the people who had drowned in Noah's day, by the way, does not mean there is a second chance for anyone else after death — this was the only group he preached to. I like to think that he did it because no one will ever be able to say God is unjust. The people who drowned in Noah's day could have said, 'Well, you weren't fair to us because you drowned us and you've never done that to any other generation.' They will never be able to say that, because Jesus went and preached to them. Nobody will ever, on judgment day, be able to look at God and say: 'God, that wasn't fair, that wasn't right.' My trust is in a God

I know well enough to be sure that whatever he does is right. Nebuchadnezzar came to the same conclusion — whatever God does is right.

People ask me about babies who die before they are old enough to believe —what happens to them? My answer is that I don't know because the Bible doesn't tell me. People say: that doesn't comfort me. If one of my children had died as a baby (and praise the Lord they didn't) I would have said to God: I know you well enough to know that whatever you do with my baby will be absolutely right. I know you well enough not to ask what you have done with my baby. We must not go beyond the word of God and give people false comfort that does not come from the word of truth. All my comfort is in this: I know God well enough to know he is never unfair, he never does anything wrong, never does anything unjust.

Now why should Jude tell us about the angels? He is saying: even the angels are not immune from God's punishment, so be careful. Do not get involved, as they did, with 'strange flesh', that is the word he uses —in other words, with forbidden sexual activity. That is putting it bluntly. He immediately, and very naturally says, my third example is Sodom and Gomorrah. Well we hardly need to say anything about that because they have given us a word in the Oxford English Dictionary: 'sodomy', which is shortened in slang to calling someone a 'sod', which is the same as the word 'bugger' —and it has all come from four towns in Israel.

Let us remember what happened. Abraham and his nephew Lot, together with their servants, are entering the promised land at last, having made a long journey to get there. All the way there has been friction between the servants of Lot and the servants of Abraham. Finally, Abraham very sensibly says an extraordinary thing: we are not getting on together, so let's go our different ways — you choose one part of the promised land, I'll go anywhere else. What an amazing thing for the uncle to let his nephew choose first. But Abraham was a man of peace, a man of beautiful spirit, and he wanted peace with his nephew. Lot looked down. You need to go to Israel to see that there is a ridge of Judean hills which are rather bare and a bit inhospitable and very cold in winter (they get snow), but less than fifteen miles from the top of the hills you are down in a deep valley which is tropical all year round. So when it is snowing in Jerusalem you can get on a bus and twenty minutes later you are in the tropics! There is no other place on earth like it. That deep valley is about fifteen hundred feet below sea level. There was a lot of tropical greenery; it looked so lush, full of palm trees, and Lot would have preferred that place to the barren hills. It was called the 'Jordan jungle', it was rich and so green and full of water. Most of it has disappeared now. So he had the valley and Abraham had the hills.

If you have ever been to America, think of choosing between Los Angeles and San Francisco or the Rocky Mountains inland. You look up at the Rockies and see snow, bare mountain tops, and then you look down at the green at the coast, at Los Angeles and San Francisco, and people want to live down on the coast — which is on top of an earthquake fault called the 'San Andreas' fault. The Jordan Valley was on top of the biggest fault in the earth's surface, which runs from Mount Hermon right down to Kenya (the Great Rift Valley). It is nearer the fire in the heart of the earth than any other point on the globe. That was where Lot chose to go, as today people live on the San Andreas fault, knowing that it is due to blow any day now. Isn't it amazing? Because it is a nicer place to live. And the same thing that happened in Sodom and Gomorrah is happening in San Francisco. It has become the gay capital of America and that was what Sodom became.

Let us see how it became that way. If we are not careful, we tend to think only of homosexuality when we think of Sodom. You are quite wrong to do that because that was not how they began. How did they begin? They were God's people, in that God created everybody. Lot and his family went there and Lot actually became an elder of the city, responsible for its morals. And here is Ezekiel: 'This was the sin of Sodom, she and her daughters were arrogant, overfed and unconcerned. They did not help the poor and needy, they were haughty and did detestable things before me.' So it started with self-centredness. It started with greed. It started with pride. It started with indifference to the poor and needy. It only *finished* in homosexuality. We do not need to rehearse all the details of the biblical account, except to remind ourselves that one day two angels, who looked like really beautiful men, went down to Sodom and they visited Lot, his wife and his two daughters. By this time the men of Sodom had reached the end of their self-indulgence and they were now indulging freely in the thing that we associate with them: sex between men and men. We are all capable of that, and Romans chapter 1 says that God just needs to take the brakes off you, and you would be doing it. So do not look down your nose at those who have got caught up in it, you could do it. It is one of the signs that God is angry with a nation that homosexuality abounds, because he just takes the brakes off and he lets people indulge themselves and do what they want. That is one of the results, and Satan is going right through our country, and making men more feminine and women more masculine. He is teaching men to wear earrings and have handbags, and he is teaching women to walk around in trousers and jackboots. He is trying to obliterate the distinction that God made between male and female, he is trying to destroy creation order, and he is killing sex and he is killing romance. It is happening before our very eyes and it happened in Sodom.

Immediately after those two beautiful men (who were actually angels) came into Lot's house, there was a crowd of men outside the door saying we want to know these men (and the word 'know' in scripture means to have sex; Adam 'knew' Eve and she conceived). We want to have sex with these two beautiful men we saw walk down the street. That even breaks the Semitic laws of hospitality, never mind anything else. But it was more serious than that. These men were beautiful, and the men wanted sex with them, so they came and clamoured. How low Lot had sunk — he said to them: Look, I'll give you my two daughters and you can rape them as much as you like, but don't touch my guests. A father who would do that to his own daughters! That tells you how much this man of God had become caught up in the whole thing. The crowd refused, they wanted the two beautiful men. And the Bible says they were doing exactly what the angels had been doing before the flood. The angels had wanted sex with men, and here were the men of Sodom wanting sex with angels. It is the same stepping out of God's boundaries and, as the Bible puts it, hankering after strange flesh. The Bible says the body of your wife belongs to you, and your body, as a husband, belongs to her — anything else is 'strange flesh'. That is what God says, that is the way he meant it to work, and that is the way that brings romance and love and beauty. The other way brings ugliness and death.

That is the third example Jude brings, and he says now: these men who have got in among you are doing all that. They are polluting their own bodies, they are defying all authority, they are a law to themselves. They even smear and make crude jokes about angels.

Then Jude remembers something else, and it is a

little story that is not in the Old Testament. Our Old Testament says that Moses died on Mount Nebo. From there you can see the length and breadth of the promised land. God said: You are not going to get into the promised land, Moses; you were among those who didn't believe, you come up with me. We are told that Moses died up on Mount Nebo all alone and was buried up there, but no man knows where his grave is. So naturally that raises a big question, doesn't it? He cannot have buried himself, so who buried him? Did you ever ask that question when you read that in the Bible? We know what happened when Moses died and his body lay there on the top of the mountain with no funeral. We know in the Bible that it is a disgrace and a shame for a body not to have a decent burial. A murderer's body was never buried. Jesus' body should never have been buried. They would have thrown it in the Valley of Hinnom — that was what they did with crucified people, they threw their bodies in the rubbish dump called Gehenna, where the worms ate it up and the fire burned it up. This was the very valley where Judas had tried to hang himself and the rope had snapped — and he had fallen down into the bottom of the Valley of Hinnom, the Valley of Gehenna, and his bowels had gushed. The scripture says: 'he went to his own place'. That was where one of the twelve disciples finished up, in the Valley of Gehenna which Jesus always said was a picture of hell. They did not throw Jesus' body into that place because a man called Joseph of Arimathea said: no, he's got to be given a decent burial, he can have my grave. And Jesus had that grave for three days. Somebody saw that Jesus was not left for the birds to pick. Surely Moses, the greatest prophet before Jesus, ought to be buried. He was buried.

So who buried him? Michael was told to bury him. So the angel who guarded Israel was told to go and bury the body. And Michael arrived on Mount Nebo to conduct the funeral and bury Moses (angels do very practical things — they cook meals, as they did for Elijah, and they can dig a grave and bury). When Michael arrived, there was Satan standing by the body. Satan said: you can't have this body, it's mine. Isn't it amazing that Satan is so perverted that even when a man is dead and gone he will try to get the body? He said this body stays here, it is not to be buried. Do you know the reason he gave? He said: Michael, this man is a murderer, he killed an Egyptian and he belongs to me and he doesn't get buried. There was Satan trying to prevent Moses, the very prophet of God, from having a decent funeral. Michael resisted the temptation to give Satan as good as he was giving, resisted the temptation to accuse him of slander. Michael was above that but also knew his place, and he knew that he was not the one to judge even Satan. He said, 'The Lord reprimand you.' Satan left, and Michael buried the body of Moses — that is the story. You say: 'Well, that's not in my Bible.' Yes it is, it is here in the epistle of Jude, so it is in the Bible. So God says it is true. Wherever Jude heard it, the Holy

Spirit would never have told Jude to put it in if it was not true. What Jude is saying is that if even the chief of the archangels, Michael himself, would not speak rudely to Satan you had better be careful about making jokes about him.

Look again at that last verse in the portion of the epistle given above. What is up with these men, what makes them tick, what is wrong with them? The answer is they abuse everything they do not understand. That is the first thing which is wrong. And I have seen people, ignorant people, who make jokes about anything they do not understand. Have you noticed that?

I heard someone using pretty colourful language, and there was quite often more than one 'damn' in his conversation. That word 'damn' is a terrible word, meaning 'to send someone to hell'. But people who do not understand these things use them as swear words. They abuse what they do not grasp, and it is a cheap thing to do. If you just criticise whatever you do not understand, you are following these men. Just because you do not understand a thing it does not mean it is something to joke about and treat with crude language. The other side of it is that the things they understand are bad things and will ruin them, because the only way they understand life is through their animal instincts.

I have worked among men and I think everybody should before they go into full-time Christian service. I am sad that so many pastors went straight from school to a theological college and then on into the pulpit. I notice that everybody Jesus called into full-time service was already in a job, trade or profession. They were fishermen, tent makers or tax collectors. These men are like some of those I worked with. I used to milk ninety cows from four o'clock every morning, with one other worker who had the dubious reputation of being the man in that area who was able to swear longest without repeating himself. He could go for some minutes in blasphemy and obscenity without ever using the same word twice. People used to egg him on to do it. What was the result? Well, I was not a Christian then and it was not long before I found I was using the same words. Like Isaiah, I became a man of unclean lips dwelling in the midst of a people of unclean lips. But that man could abuse everything sacred, whether the relationship between a man or a woman or the relationship between man and God. He could blaspheme and make obscene remarks and make everything ugly and dirty, because he did not understand any of it. He was like an animal, and what he understood were the animal instincts of his own body. That was what he lived for, and his whole conversation was in that area.

Now what was wrong in the days of Noah? What was wrong was that they were living just like animals. They were eating and drinking and mating, says Jesus, which is all the animals do. He went on to say (in Luke 17) not only in the days of Noah were they eating and drinking and mating, in the days of Lot they were eating and drinking and mating. Just looking after the desires of the flesh, that is all you need to do to have the flood come on you — live like animals; do nothing more than the animals, just keep yourself alive and have sex.

Somebody said to an American 'What time is it in America?', and he said 'sex o'clock', which was not a bad answer. It is tragic that there are people around us just living on animal instincts, just doing what the animals do, having a good feed and mating. God intended us to live in the image of God, not to live like animals. The tragedy is that in school after school it is drummed into little children's heads: you came out of the jungle; you are apes. You cannot blame those children if when they reach adulthood they behave like animals, if they have been told nothing else in school but 'You are animals'. And Jesus said there are angels in every school in the world reporting back to Father what those children are being taught. It would be better for a teacher to have a millstone hanged around his neck and be thrown in the sea than to teach lies to little children.

These are the men of God inside the fellowship: animals, men with four legs. This little book Jude has been called 'the Acts of the Apostates', which is not a bad title. There is a difference between being a backslider and being an apostate. A backslider still believes the truth but is not living that way. An apostate is someone who is twisting the truth itself, and has deliberately turned away from the truth of the word of God. And for the apostate there is no repentance (see the epistle to the Hebrews). Once you have turned away from the truth and twisted it and denied the gospel, you will never be able to repent from that position. Thank God backsliding is not as bad as that. A backslider still knows the truth even if he has slipped away from it, and there is hope of getting him back to the truth as long as he knows the truth to get back to. But a man who has twisted the truth — a man who has altered the grace of God and made it an excuse for immorality, a man who has denied that Jesus is the only Master and the only Lord, and says he is only one among others — that man should fear the final punishment of God that came on the two and a half million unbelieving Jews, that came on two hundred angels, and that came on the four cities of Sodom, Gomorrah, Admah and Zeboiim (the city of Zoar escaped.)

The location of Sodom and Gomorrah and other cities of the plain which were destroyed was at the southern end of the Dead Sea where the soil is full of bitumen, and right underneath is the fire down at the bottom of the crack that has made the Jordan Valley. From time to time that fire seeps up through the crack and explodes the bituminous soil, which releases its pocket of gas and oil (for there is oil there), and that flies up into the air and descends as fiery rain, each little drop of bitumen burning. That was what happened to Sodom, Gomorrah, Admah and Zeboiim, and the amazing thing is that the fire that destroyed those cities lasted for many centuries. Even in Jesus' day, if people walked fifteen miles down to the Dead Sea, they could still see it burning. The historian Josephus recorded it.

So the flames burning on the site of Sodom and Gomorrah were still an example of the fire of God, because over two thousand years later it was still burning, but it is not burning now because more water came into the Dead Sea, the surface rose, and it spilled over the southern end. If you go there, climb the rock called Masada and look down, and you will see a tongue of land that almost cuts the Dead Sea in half. In Arabic it is called 'the Tongue'. South of the Tongue there is a part of the Dead Sea (only about ten feet deep in this area) under which the ruins of Sodom, Gomorrah, Admah and Zeboiim lie. If you ever go there, look and fear God. Water is being taken from the Jordan, so the Dead Sea is shrinking, and a graveyard has surfaced — that is all you can see of those four cities. It will happen to San Francisco, it will happen to Los Angeles, and it will happen to London — and it is going to happen in every city of the world. 'As it was in the days of Noah,' said Jesus; 'As it was in the days of Lot,' said Jesus — it will all happen again at the end of history.

My last word on this section must be a beautiful one. Writing to the Corinthian fellowship, which was a mixed church, but a church that had the gifts of the Spirit, Paul wrote: '. . . homosexuals, adulterers, murderers, thieves, you were like that, such were some of you.' How would you like a church whose membership was made up of people like that? Paul said 'such were some of you but you were washed, you were justified, you were sanctified in Christ Jesus through the power of the Holy Spirit.' Notice he did not say such *are* some of you, he said such *were* some of you. My appeal is this: it has got to be *were* in the church, not *are* —because Sodom is right inside the church now. Did you know that? I know it is outside. I have been told that in a school library, between two and three thousand books have been withdrawn because they upheld marriage between a man and a woman, and the local authority wants marriage between a man and a man and a woman and a woman.

I like to stay with real people rather than in hotels, and on one particular occasion I was staying in a vicarage. There I found a bachelor vicar and a young man, and it became very obvious they had an unhealthy relationship. Then I discovered that another young man had died of AIDS in that vicarage two weeks earlier. That vicar was on the floor screaming and crying three days later because they wanted to take him into hospital to test him for AIDS. I do not mention that to shock you. I preached in the largest cathedral in another country and they wanted to broadcast my sermon to the entire nation. When I arrived at the cathedral I discovered there were two thousand people in the congregation, outside broadcast vans, microphones, wires everywhere. They were going to record the service and broadcast it later that day. I preached my heart out on the fear of God, and for only three minutes I spoke on homosexuality. At the end I was told the service would never be broadcast, 'because the head of religious broadcasting is known to be a practising homosexual and he'll never let that broadcast go out.' It never has.

We are talking about the church now. Jude says it has got right in, and it has. But Jesus can get it out. And it is better for you to get it out. Do not feel any embarrassment, it is better to feel embarrassment than shame later. I believe he wants to deal with a whole lot of things in love, with a surgeon's knife maybe. Get it dealt with.

We are right in the middle of the toughest part of the letter of Jude, but it is because of the toughness that the green pastures at the end will look so good. It is when you have been through the valley of the shadow and you come out into the sunshine that you appreciate how beautiful it is. Now Jude is talking about people who have wormed their way into the fellowship to which he is writing.

* * * * *

Allah, the god of Islam, is said to have 99 names. It is interesting that 'father' is not one of them and 'love' is not one of them. Our Lord Jesus Christ has 250 names and titles. Go through your Bible and make a list of them. Queen Elizabeth II has a number of titles but she is losing them one by one. When she came to the throne she was the Empress of India, but not now — that title has been lost. There is one intriguing title she has: 'Defender of the Faith'. That one was handed down from Henry VIII, who was given it by the Pope in Rome, because Henry wrote a book against Protestant theology. It was a book against Martin Luther and his rediscovery of the word of God, and the Pope was so pleased to have a king in England attacking this Protestant Luther that he granted him that title, Defender of the Faith, which has been inherited by every sovereign in England since. It was not long after he got the title that Henry VIII decided to sack the Pope and become head of the Church of England himself. Head of the Church of England — why did he do it? Why, having preached against Protestantism, did he suddenly became a Protestant? It was over the matter of divorce, which is still one of the biggest problems. It is becoming a bigger and bigger problem right inside the church. Henry VIII wanted a divorce and the Pope would not let him have one. He decided: right, we're going Protestant, then I can give myself one. He ran into some problems with his own church leaders. You may have seen that moving and challenging film *A Man For All Seasons*, in which one man, Thomas More, tried to keep the integrity of his conscience against the king playing fast and loose with doctrines. It is a magnificent film, and it raises all the questions. I would to God that her Majesty the Queen would defend the faith in the church of which she is head. It is a title. But then God does not expect the Queen to defend the faith except as one of the saints to whom the faith was once delivered. He is calling *you* to earn the title Defender of the Faith, and Jude has written appealing to Christians to defend the faith once delivered to the saints — that is what it is all about. Are you worthy of the title? Am I 'David Pawson, Defender of the Faith'? What a challenge! There is only one faith worth calling 'the faith', and it is the gospel that the apostles preached and delivered to the saints once and for all, and it is that gospel which is being destroyed in this country — and we are called to defend it. It is being watered down, and we have been seeing this all the way down the line. And now we are to learn something more about the men in the church to which Jude wrote who were watering it down, who were perverting the faith, who were making the grace of God into an excuse for sinning.

Every apostle had that problem. Whenever they preached free grace there were people who said, 'Great, I can sin; God will forgive me — that's fine, I can do what I like, he will never punish me.' That is a dreadful perversion of the faith. Paul had to deal with it. There were people who said, 'Let's sin so that God can give us more grace.' John had to deal with it. Peter had to deal with it.

I recall a Christian meeting held in a tent, when there was one particular moment when a wave of unbelief ran through the gathering. You could almost feel it! It was the moment when I raised the possibility of punishment from God for believers. It was when I spoke about what happened to the Israelites after they were redeemed from Egypt by the blood of a lamb — that the majority of them, all but two, failed to make it, and I pointed out that this incident is used again and again in the New Testament as an example of what can happen to Christians. The letter to the Hebrews says it, Paul uses it, so does Jude. They all say it is a warning that having started out does not mean you are safe until you get there. That was the moment when I saw face after face saying: 'Wrong! I am saved! I am safe! —there will be no punishment of God for me, ever.' If that is your response as you read this, I call you now, in the name of God, to repent of that unbelief. Because I will tell you what unbelief is: it started in the Garden of Eden when Satan said to Eve, 'God doesn't really mean it'. Unbelief is not atheism. Unbelief is reading the Bible and reading such letters as the letter of Jude and saying, 'God doesn't really mean it,' or, 'I'm sure he wouldn't punish me.'

It is interesting that in America an opinion poll was taken across a big cross-section of the population who were asked whether they believed in life after death, and 65% said they did. They were then asked, 'Do you believe then that you will go to heaven?' —and again 65% said yes. Then came the question, 'Do you know anyone who will go to hell?' Once more, 65% said yes, we know someone who will go to hell. It will always be someone else, and one of the incredible twists of our human mind is that we think it will never happen to us. It applies in so many areas of life. I have tried to comfort people to whom disaster has come and so often they have said, 'Pastor, I never believed this could happen to me.' How often have you heard that? Yet we know that life is precarious. We know that people are getting killed by the hundred in traffic accidents, but we believe that it will never happen to us. A lady in our church was a nurse, a hospital sister of the ward where patients died of cancer almost every day. One day they discovered she had it and she said, 'David, I never for one moment thought I could get it,' yet she had been nursing many other people.

We had an undertaker who was converted in Guildford and I asked him to give his testimony. He rose to speak, and when he said, 'I am an undertaker' the place froze —you could see people stiffen! Some people did not want to shake hands with him afterwards because he embalmed people. 'That's the reaction I get at every social occasion I go to,' he said. 'People ask me what job I do, and I say, "I am an undertaker" —then they don't want to know, because they're convinced that death will never happen to them. "Oh it can't, not to me. I couldn't die . . . !"'

That is about the only certain thing I can predict about your future unless the Lord comes back first. The undertaker continued, 'For twenty years every day I laid out dead people, and put them in the grave or in the crematorium, and I never once thought about my own death.' It is a quirk of our human minds that we will not face the truth because we do not want to think it could ever happen to us.

That is what happened when I was preaching on that occasion in the tent. I preach what I believe is the word of God. There are clear warnings in scripture — to Christians — that Christians may not make it, and that we must *go on believing*, that he may *go on keeping* us. I could take you through scripture after scripture where that is made plain. There came a day in my life when as a Bible teacher I said to God: 'God, I'm going to preach your word as far as I understand it, with the best of my ability, whether it fits in with what I already believe or not, whether the people want to hear it or not. I am prepared to believe that you mean what you say in every part of the Bible.' That was when God released something in me to preach his word, and I am more afraid of him than of you! I find that most of us have come to the Bible with a framework of thinking that we have been brought up in (whatever our denomination or tradition) and we have a kind of fixed notion of what we want to believe. Then we find something in the Bible that does not fit what we want to believe, and it is what we do then that tells us whether we are believers. Usually the bits we do not want to fit in are the passages that threaten us and make us feel vulnerable and exposed, and it is then that unbelief sets in and we say, 'Oh I'm sure it doesn't really mean that; I'm sure that's not what God meant.' So I call on you to repent of that attitude. Of course I am not saying that I am an infallible interpreter of God's word. I am not! I am still learning, but I am saying there are statements in scripture that seem pretty obvious in their meaning — statements that may not fit in with your preconceived notions or the traditions of the church in which you were brought up, but they are God's word, and somehow we must accept that God means what he says.

Satan said to Eve: 'You will not surely die . . . .' The suggestion is: God is not really like that, he would not do that to you, he loves you; he is just trying to frighten you off something he does not want you to do; he does not really mean it. Ever since then, Satan has been suggesting the same thing.

'Woe' is a biblical word we do not like. It does not fit in with our notions of a 'nice' God. Oh how we love every statement that begins with the word 'blessed'! Billy Graham called them the 'bootiful attitudes', which is not a bad paraphrase, but we love to hear 'Blessed . . .' and we pick those texts out and suck them because they are sweet, but for every time the Lord says 'blessed', he also says 'woe', and that is the opposite of 'blessed'. As the word 'blessed' brings blessing into people's lives, the word 'woe' brings curses into people's lives. But because we do not like the word it has almost dropped out of our language. Parents, when they became angry or impatient, sometimes used to say to children:'Woe betide you if . . . .' Have you heard that use of it? I have translated 'woe' here: 'Woe betide these men.' It is a curse, a sentence upon them. If you read Luke chapter 6, you will find that where Jesus said 'Blessed are the poor', he added 'but woe to you rich,' and by New Testament standards almost everybody in the UK is rich. He said, 'Woe to you rich', and one of the reasons that the gospel is not having free rein in this country is because we are so rich and comfortable. When he said 'Blessed are you who mourn,' he immediately added 'but woe to you who laugh' — and when did you hear a sermon on that verse? Probably never.

Bethsaida, the home of the fishermen, is just round the corner from Capernaum in the Galilee. In Jesus' day there were five large towns around five miles of coast, forming a heavily populated area. Now there is not a soul living in four of those five cities. Tiberias is still there and is home to tens of thousands, but at Bethsaida you have to hunt through the grass and you find a few little black basalt stones which are all that is left. Just a little further up the slope, you find a few more black rocks, and that is all that remains of Korazin. You can walk back along the coast and you find some ruins (again, in the black hard basalt rock of the area) which is all that is left of Capernaum, and nobody is living there now. Now why is Tiberias still there and none of the other cities? Because our Lord Jesus pronounced 'Woe' to Bethsaida and Korazin; and he said that Capernaum would go down to the depths (see Matthew 11:20ff).

'Woe' was not just a word used by the Old Testament prophets, it was a word that is frequently on Jesus' lips, and when he talked about religious leaders, he said, 'Woe to you who like the chief seats', 'Woe to you who like to dress up in robes and be looked up to and became rabbi, woe to you.' That is a curse, and so we need to listen every time the word 'woe' comes in scripture. It is a shocking word.

There was a man who went into the temple of God and prayed, and he saw the holiness of God and he said, 'Woe is me, because these lips blasphemed and I dwell in the midst of people of unclean lips. Woe, I'm cursed' — and he saw an angel flying straight for him with a big pair of tongs, with a red hot live coal from the altar. That was not a vision. This was a real, red hot, live coal and the angel flew straight for his mouth and burnt it —and for the rest of his life Isaiah had a scarred mouth. When he got up to preach people said, 'How did you get a mouth like that?' And Isaiah could say that God had cauterised his mouth before he could preach his word.

When I was a little boy, one of my biggest problems was nose bleeding. It was embarrassing. It happened in the worst places at the worst times. I had to press the back of my neck and lie down, and it made a mess of everything. Finally, when I was about twelve years old, the family doctor said, 'We'll have to cauterise that.' I didn't know that big word and I said, 'What do you mean, what's that?'

He said, 'It's alright, we just burn up the veins inside your nostril and it stops.'

I thought, 'You're not going to burn my veins.' But I was so fed up with it.

He said, 'Do you want to go on with this or do you want me to cure it?'

So I went to his surgery and he said, 'Lie on that couch,' and then he got a thing that looked like a portable welding outfit and he set it up and plugged it in. Then he came for me with this thing and he stuck it up that right nostril and I could smell steak! It was horrible and it was me on the grill, not steak! —and since that day I have been free. The Lord wants to cauterise. He is wanting to take a red hot coal and touch that thing so you can be free. 'Woe is me . . . I am a man of unclean lips', Isaiah said —but the Lord had not finished with him. He was going to burn those lips and then tell him what to say.

So we can understand this— woe is me because I have used my mouth to curse people. But Paul said: Woe is me if I preach not the gospel. There is a curse on a preacher who will not tell others the blessed truth. 'Woe' is a very important word.

Now we touch on another feature of these men who are corrupting the faith. There is a process of four stages going on in Jude's epistle. (1) They corrupt the creed; (2) They corrupt their conduct; (3) Now, they corrupt their character; (4) That will corrupt their conversation. That is the process of corruption which is going on here. When your faith is twisted your behaviour will be twisted because we behave as a result of how we believe. Whatever we believe, that is how we will behave. Our theology affects our ethics. Sentimental theology produces situational ethics. I am sorry if you do not understand that, but you will come to. Situational ethics does not say what is right and wrong, but asks: what is the situation? Jesus simply said that whoever divorces his wife and marries another commits adultery, and whoever marries a divorcee commits adultery, and if a wife divorces her husband and remarries she commits adultery. And Paul said: if you have to separate from your partner, then remain single and unmarried, or seek to be reconciled to your partner. That is basic biblical teaching. There is only one exception to this, in one text in the New Testament, and I will not discuss divorce and remarriage with anyone until they are prepared to start from the rights and wrongs that Jesus laid down. But what happens? As soon as I talk to anyone in this matter, they say, 'Well, this is our situation.' I then ask, 'But do you accept the rights and wrongs first?'

'Let me tell you our situation,' they say. 'Let me tell you how it happened,' or, 'Let me tell you that I wasn't a Christian before' —as if starting from the situation is going to find the right way out. This is simply an illustration. As soon as you start with a situation and then try to find your way to what is right, you will get confused. If you start with what is right and wrong, then look at your situation in the light of that, you will come to the Lord's will for you. Now you know what situational ethics is, and Henry VIII was right into situational ethics. That is why he went through six wives. That is how he thought from his situation instead of from the word of God. We are always getting ourselves into a situation and then trying to justify it, trying to find some loophole in scripture. The single exception that Jesus made to the rules has been stretched and stretched until anybody can try to persuade me from their situation that they can squeeze through that loophole and justify it from scripture.

Once you have corrupted the creed and corrupted theology and belief, it is only a step to corrupting your conduct, and once you have corrupted your conduct you are on the way to corrupting your character because your character is the result of your conduct. Your habitual way of reacting in situations produces your character, so from an act we reap our habits, from our habits we reap our character, and from our character we reap our destiny. And how do you find out what kind of a character a person has? It comes out in their conversation, and the quickest way to find out what a man is really like is to listen to how he talks. That is the progression. If you have right beliefs, you will then produce right behaviour, and that will produce the right character, and that will produce the right conversation. But the whole thing can go wrong. Once you twist the faith, you twist conduct, then you twist character, and finally it comes right out in your conversation. Jesus said, 'Whatever is in a man comes out of his mouth.' Their speech betrays them! If you wonder whether a man has twisted the creed, listen to the way he talks, and it will come out in his speech because that is his character. The things we say, especially when we are not really thinking, especially when we are under pressure, are the things that reveal our character, which is why Jesus said, 'For every idle word man will be brought into judgment.' Do you realise that God has a tape recording of everything you ever said? I know in my own life that would be enough to damn me to hell. If I had never committed any other sin, my speech would betray me because my speech reveals what I am.

Let us look first at character. Jude, fond as he is of everything in threes, takes three men from the Old Testament and just says: Look at those men —that is the character of the men who are now troubling you. Cain is the first. The element in Cain's character that made him do what he did was anger. Then he mentions Balaam, and the element in his character that made him do what he did was avarice. Then he mentions Korah and the element in his character that made him do what he did was ambition. These three things are the marks of men who twist the creed —anger, avarice and ambition.

Consider Cain. He and Abel brought their offering to the Lord in worship. Cain brought an offering from the crops of the field; Abel brought fat animals he had killed because he was a stock breeder, and they offered the results of their work to the Lord, and the Lord said, 'I'll accept Abel's offering but not Cain's, that is the wrong offering.' Why did God not accept that one? He told Cain quite directly, 'You didn't do right. If you'll do right, I'll accept you.' What does he mean — that he had not done right in the rest of his life, or that he was not doing right in what he had brought? There is a very simple answer to this. They must both have been told by their parents the story of their parents' sin and what followed, and they must have been told by their parents fig leaves were no use. God had to kill some animals to cover us. From the very first pair of human beings, blood has been involved in putting things right between men and God. That is a principle that goes right through from the first chapters of Genesis to the cross of Calvary. Blood is necessary. It costs blood to get through to God. And because you do not go to church with a little lamb or a pigeon under your arm for your church leader to take a knife and slaughter, that is not because the principle has changed, it is because Jesus has done all that was needed. Otherwise you would have to go and get a lamb or a pigeon before you dared to come to God, because without blood you cannot get near him. Cain brought the fruit of his work but he did not bring any blood. There would be no death. Now why?

There is very little indication in Genesis itself but we have some other books that enlarge on that whole incident, and we have already seen that Jude looks for truth in other books as well, where it is truth and where the Holy Spirit guides, and there is a remarkable Jewish Targum about this very story of Cain and Abel.

It records a conversation between them in which Cain's first reaction is, 'God isn't fair. God isn't just to accept yours and not mine.' From that first anger against God, Cain then goes on to argue: 'And there will be no day of judgment and there's no justice in this world or the next, and there will be no judge and no punishment for the wicked and no reward for the righteous. I just don't believe in the principle of judgment.'

Abel replies: 'But there is a Judge and there is punishment and there is reward.' I am not going to vouch for that story, but I believe it has got to the heart of Cain's thinking. Cain's anger is against the justice of God. He is saying, 'God is unjust. The world is unjust. How can there be judgment in such an unfair world?' Which is exactly how other people talk. Have you noticed how often sinners say, 'God is unfair. If I were God, I wouldn't do that. If I were God I wouldn't let earthquakes happen. If I were God I wouldn't let the children in Ethiopia starve.'

I was in Australia and put through twenty-five minutes on the radio by one interviewer. He really gave me such a rough time that I had letters from Australians apologising for his treatment of me — not Christians but ordinary listeners. There was a bitterness in him, and he said, 'How can God allow the Ethiopian children to starve? How can there be a good God, a just God, and allow that to happen?' He had recently been to Ethiopia and he had reported on it on the radio, and he thought he had really got me pinned down. I replied, 'Listen, in the very same newspaper that I read about the starving children in Ethiopia for the first time, on the same page of the same newspaper in the very next column was the report of the United Nations Food Organisation which said that in 1984 there was such a bumper corn harvest in the whole world that there was 13% more corn in the world than the whole world population needed.' I said, 'Don't you dare blame God for that. He did his bit. What earthly father could blame God, if that earthly father starved his own children while the larder was full of food? Let's put the blame where the blame lies, on the selfishness of a world in which 18% of the population eat 86% of the world's food — and the 18% includes us!'

You see, people are so prone to say, 'God's not fair', and as soon as they have said that, they jump on to say, '. . . and there can't ever be justice, even in the next world; there's no judgment; there's no punishment.' That is the essence of unbelief: that God will never punish sin. 'Oh, God would never punish me.' Don't you believe it! Unbelief says that God did not really mean it when he said the wages of sin is death; that God did not really mean it that you can 'make shipwreck of your faith'; that God did not really mean it that having tasted the powers of the age to come and then turning your back on Jesus there can be no repentance whatever for that. 'Oh, God didn't really mean that, surely?'

But this is written by Judas, the brother of Jesus, and there was another Judas who lived for three years with Jesus, who preached and taught and healed in the name of Jesus, who went out as a missionary for Jesus for three whole years, but avarice was eating into his heart. He was the treasurer and he could not keep his hands out of the till. It was his undoing in the end — and Jesus himself could not stop it. I am glad that we have an example of someone who is as far in as that, because it is our business to say 'Lord is it I?' Just someone sitting at the Last Supper whom Satan entered into — and 'it was night'. What a terrible phrase that is. Black. That is Cain, the man who picked up from his mother that God did not really mean it. The very same thought that occurred to Eve occurred to Cain. 'Oh, God won't really punish me.' And God said, 'Cain, I'm warning you. If you don't do what's right, sin is crouching at the door.' God knew that if Cain went on with this anger, he would become a murderer, and he did, and the first murder of history happened in the first family — through envy, the same motive that was responsible for the worst murder in history, the death of Jesus. Pilate saw that. For envy and this inner anger is there in men who twist the gospel. There is an inner resentment, a feeling of unfairness directed at God, and therefore a rejection of the justice of God and of the punishment of God.

The widespread notion right through this land that God is a 'nice old God who will never punish anyone' is an absolute lie from hell. Some Christians seem more afraid of demons than of God. They are more afraid of something happening that would disturb them than of

God dealing with them. Why should we be more afraid of everything else but God?

We live not far from Greenham Common. Those poor women were there because they feared the bomb more than anything else and were living under polythene sheeting for two or three years. Some of them were away from their families so long their husbands divorced them, the children didn't see them. They were there because their mortal fear was that somebody was going to press the button and wipe us off the face of the earth — and the peace movement grew tremendously all over the world, in Europe particularly, as people panicked about the bomb. I believe what Jesus said about the bomb. 'Don't fear the one who can kill your body and after that do nothing more to you. Rather fear him who after death can destroy your body and soul in hell.' Listen, fear of the nuclear destruction, if that is at the top of your agenda, is not at the top of God's agenda. I know that no man will be able to press the button and end this world. There is a finger already on the button and it is the finger of Jesus. No man can open the scroll and break the seals and start the countdown to the end of history except the Lamb who is the Lion of the tribe of Judah. Nobody can do it but Jesus, and Jesus will bring history to an end in his own time and in his own way. That is why I do not fear the bomb, but I do fear the one who can do worse than the bomb can do to you. That is a healthy fear.

What about the sin of Balaam, that was due to

avarice? We have read in Jude about men who are like brute beasts without the capacity for reason, but I have the feeling that some animals have more sense than men, including Balaam's ass. Do you know animals can respond to things? They know when an earthquake is coming. You watch the animals! They know it before men do, and Balaam's ass knew there was an angel in the middle of the road before Balaam did, and God gave that animal the power of speech. Donkeys laugh anyway. That is about all many Christians know about Balaam, but do read the whole story.

Balaam was hired by Balak of the Moabites to curse Israel. They had camped at the edge of Moab, and the king of Moab was a bit worried about that, and he got hold of Balaam, a prophet. He knew he had supernatural power and said, 'Would you use it against Israel and curse them, and I'll make it worth your while?' Balaam could not curse Israel because God would not let him, but he wanted that money. So how could he get it? He went to Balak. To summarise the account, the reply was: I can't curse Israel, God won't let me, but I can think of a way that might be pretty useful to you, to get rid of them. They have a weakness for pretty girls. Send a few girls in among them and you will be able to undermine their morals, and you'll get them involved in things that God won't approve of. Now, how about that for a suggestion? What is it worth to you, Balak?

For avarice he found a way of bringing the Israelites into immorality, and through that into idolatry, so that he brought them down and he led to the death of many. He was a murderer like Cain. Avarice murders just as anger does. That is why Jesus said, 'You've heard it said, "You shall not kill", but don't you be angry with anyone because that is as much murder, wishing them dead could get you to hell.' That is the story of Balaam, and these men had wormed their way into the fellowship Jude is writing to. They had a desire to be supported financially. They were thinking of the money they could make.

Then what about Korah? When God appointed Moses and Aaron as leaders, Korah would not accept the leadership. He wanted his own show and he got 250 people to form an underground group with him. That was not the last time such a thing happened! And dear Moses said: I'll leave you to judge. We'll gather tomorrow morning and we'll see what you say, God. That is a wise approach. The next morning they all gathered, 250 with Korah, and Moses and Aaron and the rest. Moses said, 'Keep well back from them because God is going to decide,' and as they watched, the earth trembled and opened up and 250 people fell, and it closed and they disappeared.

Now what did these three men, Cain, Balaam and Korah, have in common? They were all self-willed, and because they were, it led many others to death. They were murderers, and that is the nature of these people Jude is warning them about. It will come out in their speech and he lists certain things whereby you can identify such men. First of all, they are pretty good at finding fault. They are always complaining. Nothing is ever good enough for them. That reminds me of a Jewish joke. A Jewish wife gave two ties to her husband for his birthday, and he came down wearing one of them. She looked down and said, 'What was wrong with the other one?' There are people you cannot win with. They are grumbling. They are discontented. Whatever you do for them is wrong, yet on the other hand you will also find them constantly flattering themselves and flattering other people when it is to their advantage. You listen to this kind of talk and you know what kind of a character is in there, and you know what kind of conduct is going on behind the scenes, and you know what kind of creed they have. It all comes through to that sort of conversation. It comes out in their speech and it is a dirty heart that produces dirty speech. It is a twisted heart that produces twisted speech.

Let us draw threads together. In a series of vivid pictures Jude outlines the character of these men. He says they are like submerged rocks that could wreck everything. What a picture! Under the surface, you are not really aware of how dangerous they are — but they could wreck your fellowship.

Jude particularly talks about the love feast they have. Now in the early church communion was not a ceremony. The Lord's Supper was part of an ordinary meal. I wish we could do that again. We used to do it in our church in Guildford. We had a meal, with little tables. All the church members gathered round with just a piece of bread and a cup of wine in the middle, and after we had had a good meal and lots of fellowship, at each table someone would give thanks for the bread and pass it to the other, and somebody would give thanks to God. It is a beautiful thing to do. Have you ever tried it? It is how they did it in the early church. It was a meal and it was a love feast, and they loved each other and they would hug and kiss each other. Now that is fine, but when you have men like these in among you, it is dangerous. There is a difference between a kiss and a holy kiss. Do you know the difference? Two minutes! I leave you to think that one through. Young people know what I am talking about. But when you have men who, as we have learned, have wrong desires for other men, to say nothing of the ladies, you let them into a love feast and you are playing with fire. They are like submerged rocks and it is very easy to slip over the line in all the huggy, kissy fellowship we are having now.

They are not just like submerged rocks, they are like clouds. Now if you live in the Middle East, you live for the clouds. When the wind is from the east there are no clouds, the hot, dry desert wind comes and dries up the grass. In hours the grass disappears and the flower fades, so you long and pray for the wind from the west, from the Mediterranean. You might look out to the west — maybe from the top of Mount Carmel as Elijah's servant did, and you see a cloud no bigger than a man's hand. I have stood on Carmel and seen a cloud that I could cover with my fist at arm's length, but I have known that rain is going to come — because when clouds begin to form over the Mediterranean, and the wind is from the west, and the cloud grows and grows, like Elijah you run for shelter because that cloud is going to bring rain. But when the wind is terribly strong, even from the west, it blows those clouds straight past and there is no rain. These men are like clouds driven so hard by the wind they drop no rain —full of promise but no performance; full of claims but never producing anything; big mouths, swollen opinions of themselves. They are not only like that. What else are they like? Uprooted trees in the autumn. Why are they uprooted? Because they have neither had leaves nor fruit on them. They were planted hoping that they would bear fruit. None!

Next, Jude says they are like wild waves. You see this wave coming, 'a real dumper' as they say in Australia. It comes and it grows and it crashes on the beach with a great noise. Then it disappears, and what is left? Dirty foam! Have you ever seen that happen? And these men are like big waves and you think there are going to be tremendous things happening, but they depart and just leave dirty, foaming shame. They are like shooting stars which are so spectacular. 'Look, there's a shooting star' — and it has gone. It draws all the attention but you cannot do anything with a shooting star. It disappears into blackness for ever and you cannot guide your life by it. You can navigate by the stars (they did even in

Bible times) but you can only navigate by stars that stay in their courses and are stable. Do not navigate by a shooting star! By the time you have turned after it, it has gone, and these men are like shooting stars. They are stars and suddenly they are big names and everybody's attention is on them, and they are gone, so if you guide your life by them, you are very foolish.

What a picture of the character of these men. How foolish to follow such people. Jude says that you should have expected men like these in the church. It was not unexpected. The prophets and the apostles said it would happen. Why did you forget that? All the liberalising that is coming into the church right now —the first prophet in history who foretold that was Enoch. The apostle said it would happen — in the last days there will come scoffers. We have got to expect this. It is not a surprise to God. It is not even a surprise to those who know their Bible. Wherever the truth is preached, Satan will try to pervert it because he knows he will never destroy the church from the outside, he can only destroy it from the inside, and that is why you can expect people subtly to twist the creed and then to twist conduct and say: 'It's okay to sin because God forgives you', and then to twist their character so they become full of promise but with no performance, and you will know it by their conversation. They are fault finding toward others —and there is flattery of themselves and flattery of others when they stand to gain by it. They step on the faces of those below them and lick the boots of those above them to get up the ladder. Anger, avarice and ambition are what make them tick, and yet they talk about the grace of God. They come to communion. They speak about Jesus Christ, but never as the only Jesus, just as one among others — and never of the grace of God that is given to you so that you can live a holy life.

We do not know very much about Enoch, except that he was a great walker. Every day of his life he went walking, and one day he went walking so far he walked right into heaven. As one preacher put it, it is as though at the end of the day God said to him: You have walked a long way today, Enoch; you are a long way from home, you might as well come and stay with me — and that was what happened. Fancy that, he never died! No undertaker measured him up. There was no coffin, no grave, because he just went on walking right into glory. God is a God who walks. That is one of many surprising things the Bible reveals about God. Another thing is that he whistles. That is in Isaiah (twice in the first eight chapters). Another is that he sings — he rejoices over us with singing, and we sing because we are made in his image. And have you read in the Bible that God laughs? God walks — right from the beginning of the Bible where it says Adam heard the sound of the Lord God walking. God is a mobile God, he is on the move, and if you do not keep on the move you will lose him, because our God is walking. He is not static.

When I went to Bangkok, I went to see the temple of 1,000 Buddhas. The biggest one weighs about 30 tons and is covered with gold leaf. There it sits, and as I looked at all these Buddhas, I thought of a verse in Isaiah: 'They have eyes but they cannot see. They have ears but they cannot hear. They have mouths but they cannot talk and they have feet but they cannot walk.' I looked at all these statues of Buddha and thought: he could do with a good walk — but he can't, he's dead! God is a God who walks, and a godly man is a man who walks with God, and walking with God means that you are going in the same direction as God, and you are going at the same speed as God. You are travelling through life with God and you cannot sit down! There are too many Christians sitting on the premises, never mind standing on the promises, but actually we are called to work, to walk. When you get to heaven, do you think you are going to sit in a big armchair with 'RIP' embroidered on it? Never! It says we are going to walk in heaven. When Jesus came to show us what God was like, he walked. Most of his teaching, most of his miracles, were in the way while he walked, and he walked mile after mile after mile. If you want to know what God is like, look at Jesus — and you will see someone who walks. Even after his resurrection. What is the most famous resurrection account? — the walk to Emmaus. But what you may not have noticed is that, after he ascended back to heaven and sat down at the right hand of God the Father, he got up again and started walking. And a picture of the ascended Jesus in Revelation is of one who is walking among the lampstands. Did you ever notice that? When we get to heaven we are going to walk with him. We shall walk in white clothes with him, so don't think you are going to sit down and rest in heaven, it is not a retirement home. What a place! We will be able to walk anywhere in the universe then, because we shall have bodies like Jesus which can go into space without a spacesuit, and we shall walk with God. Enoch was a man like that, and therefore he could walk straight into heaven. He had gone the same direction as God all his life. He had walked at the same speed as God. He kept up with God. He had not run ahead of him, had not lagged behind him. So Enoch was one of the few men who never actually experienced the loneliness of dying.

Now that man, in the seventh generation after Adam, was the very first prophet on earth, the first man to speak a direct word from God. Did you know that? And his prophecy was about God coming to judge godlessness. So, right at the very beginning, the very first prophecy ever given to a man was a prophecy that God will not let godlessness continue forever. He will come and deal with it, he will bring ten thousand angels to deal with it — and the word 'godless' came into the prophecy. He is coming to put the whole human race on trial. God is coming to deal with the godless people who have godless deeds in their godless life with their godless talk. 'Godless' is Jude's key word for the whole letter.

What is godlessness? It is not irreligion. It is religion without God. It is Christianity without God. A magazine researched to find out which was the most irreligious nation on earth. They used the word 'godless', and they came to the conclusion that it was Japan, because they said there is less religion in modern materialist Japan, which has got so wrapped up in cars, television sets and electronic gadgetry, that it has become the most irreligious nation in the world. The UK was the second nation. That is our record. I think the magazine was using the wrong measuring standard because 'godless' in the Bible does not mean that you don't talk about God or don't believe in him. It means you don't know him as he really is, and therefore you don't fear him. That is all. These men that Jude was talking about talked about God. They talked about the grace of God. They talked about Jesus. They claimed to have the Spirit. Jude called them dreamers, meaning that they were claiming to have special inspiration in dreams from the Holy Spirit of God. So people would have said they were godly men — but they were not, they were 'godless' because they did not fear God, they did not believe that God punished immorality. They believed that they were safe, and therefore they are called godless.

On the night the Titanic sailed on its maiden voyage from Southampton, the captain of the ship said to the press reporters, 'God himself couldn't sink this ship.' That is godlessness. He believed in God but he did not believe God could or would do such a thing. Past Archbishops of Canterbury and York respectively said that God could not and would not burn York

Minster. That is godlessness. Do you understand what godlessness is now? And there is godlessness right through the church. Oh, there is plenty of God talk, plenty of talk about Christ, but there is an absence of the fear of God. There is a distorted view of God that does not take God seriously. Godlessness — unbelief — is to say that God does not mean what he says. It is also saying God does not mind what we do. Those two things together make up what the Bible means by 'godlessness'. If you are thinking like that, you are godless. You don't know God. You don't have a personal knowledge of him, and Paul says (in 2 Thessalonians 1) that when Jesus comes in blazing fire with his angels, he is coming to deal with two groups of people: those who don't know God and those who don't obey the gospel. It does not say he is directly coming to deal with murderers, thieves, adulterers and the rest. It says he is coming to deal with those who don't know God and don't obey the gospel. Everybody in the world has had a chance to know God. Paul says, 'Men are without excuse. The things of God are clearly seen in the creation outside us, in the conscience within us.' We ought to know there is a power greater than ourselves and we ought to know that power is concerned with right and wrong. He has planted his law in our conscience. Every man is in touch with creation and conscience and has no excuse for not knowing God, and those who have heard the gospel but not obeyed it have no excuse for not obeying the gospel — and those two groups will be dealt with. We are not to deal with the evil in the world, the angels will. Christians are often tempted to get into 'weed pulling'. Do you know what I mean by that? We are so anxious to clean this world up for God that we say, 'God, we're going to pull the weeds up.' The owner of the field says, 'Don't pull the weeds up, you might destroy the wheat.' When the harvest is ripe, the angels, says Jesus, will come. They are the reapers, not us. We are the labourers, to produce the harvest. It is the angels who will come and take the tares out of the harvest field which is the world — not the church. They will take out of the world everyone who does evil and everything that causes evil, and throw the weeds on the fire.

In fact, by the grace of God we are called to turn weeds into wheat. When I went to Winnipeg, I was intrigued. They put me on television as soon as I arrived. I happen to have read a bit of the history of Winnipeg and discovered to my astonishment that an ancestor of mine had founded that city by emptying the Scottish highlands of people to make room for sheep, and sending them off to the Red River. So I said, 'I'm happy to be here because you wouldn't be here but for my family, so I'm really interested to be here.' That really got them listening, even the cameramen. But I said: 'In the early days, the pioneers came here and they established the city, and the next group to come along were the prostitutes, and the women came to take the money off the pioneers. The next groups to come along were the families, and then after the families came the evangelists and the pastors to start churches, and that was how the mid-west towns were established. Then the churches decided to have a united anti-evil crusade, run the prostitutes out of Winnipeg and close down the red light district. All the churches rose up in enthusiastic union. They did it, and they cleaned the town up and the women moved further west, and all the Christians thought this was a great victory. I am not sure that the Lord thought it was. They pulled the weeds up, but Christians did not go to those prostitutes and tell them of the love of God. The gospel is not getting rid of them that way — and not one preacher preached to the men who had been their customers to tell them to repent.'

If we are not careful we are going to get into a 'weed pulling' crusade in this country and think that that is Christianity. Think that through very carefully. The Lord will come with his angels to deal with godlessness and we must look for his coming and pray for it, and leave judgment to him. Our task is the task of getting people saved and making sure there is wheat growing, because the wheat and the weeds will both grow together. Some Christians talk as if the church is going to get so strong we are going to push Satan across the English Channel. He can go to France and they can cope with him — as if we are going to clean up England! We are not. The kingdom of Satan is going to get stronger in England. There are other Christians, who are natural pessimists and take the opposite view, saying, 'Oh, we're in the last days. Aren't things terrible? Things are going down and down — in fact, when the Lord comes back, there could be only you and me, and I'm not sure if you're sound.' Have you heard that kind of talk? I am a realist who believes with Jesus that both are going to grow together — the kingdom of God is going to get stronger and the kingdom of Satan is going to get stronger, and there will be an increasing battle between them and increasing confrontation, until finally Jesus Christ and Antichrist face each other, and I know who is going to win because that is when Jesus will come with ten thousand angels. He has not told the church to establish the kingdom. The angels will establish it finally, but Jesus has told us to get on and announce it, and get everybody we can into the kingdom. That is a balance which is needed in Christian thinking.

Now Enoch was a great prophet. He prophesied what he did, I believe, because it was in the days of Jared, Enoch's father, that the angels had come down in the Mount Hermon area and had sex with the women and produced the monsters. So it was Enoch's generation which saw that demonic generation born, and Enoch knew that God would have to deal with it. He knew that God, while he is amazingly patient, must deal with godlessness even among the angels, and that is why he predicted the coming of the Lord with his angels to deal with godlessness. Then Enoch, at the age of sixty-five, fathered a little boy and he wondered what to call him. He had a prophetic word from God and called the boy

Methuselah. It means in Hebrew 'in the day that he dies it will come', and Enoch knew that God would come and judge that generation on the day that his boy died. What a name to give a little boy — 'In the day you die it will happen' — and it is a proof of God's patience that Methuselah lived longer than anyone else. Nine hundred and sixty-nine years that boy stayed on earth, but the day he died was the day the rains started for Noah's flood, did you know that? Isn't the Bible fascinating when you get into it? Enoch, the prophet, said: 'God is going to deal with this godlessness and he has revealed to me that he will deal with it the day my son dies', and in fact Enoch had a grandson called Noah, so now you have the whole story. God, when he says something, does it —and Jesus said, 'As in the days of Noah, so it will be in the days of the coming of the Son of Man.' God's prophetic warning has been going out over the years now and it is going to happen again. God is coming with ten thousand of his angels to deal with godlessness.

That was Enoch's prophecy which Jude writes about, and then he refers to another prophecy made by the apostles, telling us that God will deal with the godlessness of the last days. There are men who are bound to come and pour scorn on godliness. That is happening in our day too, but I want to just say a little thing to get it balanced up. I hear a lot of preachers saying, 'We're in the end times.' That is true, but the last days began at Pentecost and we have been in them ever since. The apostle said that in the last days there will be scoffers at godliness and there have been for two thousand years. The fact that we are seeing them in our day does not make our day special, nor does it tell us that we are in the very last days. Do not get confused, look for the signs that Jesus said would indicate the last, last days. He gave us four signs to look for, of which I can only see one and a half thus far, but with the speed of world events the other two and a half could come rapidly.

The men Jude is warning about are not spiritual. The flesh cannot reconcile. The apostles taught that whilst such men may have some appeal to the mind, they do not have the Spirit. It needs supernatural discernment today to discern between these two, and to know when we are actually getting sensual in our worship and ceasing to be spiritual. I find Christians are jolly good at shouting 'Hallelujah!' when you attack people far away outside the church, but I say it again, the time has come for judgment to begin with the household of God. The fire of God from heaven fell in Britain, not on a brothel, not on an abortion clinic, not on a gambling den — it fell on a cathedral, and if you miss the meaning of that, you do not know God. God's concern is to get his church back to what it ought to be so that the nation may be saved.

3

LIVING IN THE PRESENT
Read 17–23

So what can we do about this whole situation, this corruption of the Creed that has led to a corruption of conduct, that has led to a corruption of character, that has led to a corruption of conversation —because we are all aware how much it is pressing in on the church and comes up inside the church one way and another, and it has so sapped the strength of the church that we cannot save the nation.

Jude finishes in a very practical way by telling us what to do. When I began preaching (in 1947), there was a dear man who I felt was the best preacher I had ever heard and I wanted to preach like him. I will never forget what he said to me: 'David, never finish preaching without telling people what to do about it.' Wasn't that beautiful advice? Do not leave them up in the clouds. Do not leave them all gooey-eyed. Tell them what to do. And Jude, like a good preacher, tells us what to do.

The fascinating thing is he does not start by telling us what to do with these false men. He does not say burn them. He does not say turn them out. He does not say shut them up. In fact he does not say anything about them. Mind you, I believe that his letter would have finished them off altogether! Can you imagine a church getting this letter still listening to men like that? I think his letter had dealt with it. But essentially his teaching is: I am concerned about you yourselves, and the people these teachers have misled, and I am going to tell you what to do about these two groups.

Firstly, when this situation arises, when this corruption has set in, when the faith is being watered down, when anything goes and people are abusing the grace of God — when all this happens, the first thing is to do something about *yourselves*. Make sure about yourself first. Before you try to tackle anyone else, make sure that you are what you ought to be yourself; and in the little bit of advice he gives to us, that we are to build ourselves up to keep ourselves in the love of God, to pray in the Spirit, to wait patiently for the coming of the Lord, he is primarily saying you must be right before you can ever put a situation right. Now that is a profound principle which is the reason for the letter of Jude and the reason for my burden. God is saying: church, put yourself right and then you can put the world right.

What is praying in the Spirit? It is praying the way the Holy Spirit teaches you to pray, and one of the easiest ways to learn to pray in the Spirit is to pray in tongues. That is one of the great gifts of God, that he wants to give you when he baptises you in his Spirit, so that you can pray in the Spirit when you do not know how to pray, when you do not know what to pray for, when you do not know what to say next or how to keep going. You will find that praying in tongues is the answer, and Paul, the great missionary, said, 'I thank God I pray in tongues more than you all.' I often wondered how he coped with stoning and shipwreck and being beaten and all that he went through. I know now. He edified himself by praying in the Spirit. Yet I have read book after book on the life of Paul that never mentioned that that was the secret of how he built himself up! That is why you should covet that gift and ask for it. It is not a gift to be used in public except under strict limits (two or three at the most, and always interpreted, otherwise it is no use to anybody else), but what a gift to use in private. If Paul did it more than the Corinthians, he must have done it some, mustn't he? But in private. Mind you, when he was chained to a Roman soldier for twenty-four hours a day I am not surprised the guard got converted — if Paul prayed in tongues more than them all. Can you imagine being chained to Paul for eight hours? Writing a letter from prison, 'They of Caesar's household salute you.' There is no stopping an evangelist! Was it Billy Bray in Cornwall who said, 'If they put me in a barrel and threw me over the cliff, I'd shout "Hallelujah!" through the bunghole'? You cannot keep a good man down. The word of God is not bound. Build yourselves up in your holy faith, pray in the Spirit and wait for Jesus to come back — and keep yourself in the love of God. This is extremely important. It is one thing to fall in love, it is another thing to stay in love. The late Dr W. E. Sangster put a beautiful dedication in one of his books. It was entitled *The Pure in Heart* and the dedication was: 'To my wife, with whom it is as easy to stay in love as it was to fall in love.' That must go down in history as one of the most beautiful things a man ever said about his wife. Keep yourselves in love with God.

Well how do you do that? We know the modern idea of marriage is that you fall in love and you live happily ever after. There was a beautiful misprint in a romantic novel: 'They got married, and they lived happily even after.' Nice little misprint that, but if you have been married you will understand. We know that marriage has to be cultivated. Love does not just happen. How do you keep love up? Well it might be embarrassing to go into the details, but how? Have you ever had a little note from your wife on the kitchen table late one night, 'Your supper is in the dog and your slippers are in the fridge and I've gone to bed with a headache'! I will tell you: the simplest way is to consider the wishes of the one you love. That is how you cultivate it. And Jesus said, 'If you keep my commandments, you will stay in my love.' That is what the word 'abide' means. Do you want to stay in my love? Then do what I tell you. Simple as that! Fulfil the wishes of the beloved one. Is that simple enough for you? Stay in love with the Lord. Do what he tells you and the false teachers cannot touch you.

Finally, make sure that you live by hope. We have lived through an age called an 'existential' age. In simple language, that means living for today, forgetting about yesterday and forgetting about tomorrow. 'Live for every experience you can get now. It must be instant. You must have it now. You must be able to have it immediately whether it is instant coffee or instant 'love' — but live for today. The only meaning to life is your present existence, the moment now.'

Now I can understand unbelievers doing that because they are so afraid. It is a short term policy. It is the 'Esau syndrome'. Esau said, 'I'm hungry now. I'd rather have a plate of soup now than an inheritance later.' He regretted it afterwards and sought repentance with tears, but he never got back to where he had been. The 'now' generation is with us. But the believer must never think like that. The believer says, 'I am living for the day Jesus gets back. So I live for the future, not for the present.' It is true that we have wonderful foretastes of eternal life now, but we are living for immortality and we are not going to lose that for a bowl of soup today. This is a vital dimension.

False teachers promise you everything now, true teachers do not. I love the honesty of Jesus. False teachers will say, 'You can have everything you want now; by faith you can have a big house; by faith you can have a big car; by faith you can have this, that and the other.' I prefer the honesty of Jesus. He said that no man who has lost house or family or friends will not be repaid a hundredfold, with persecutions. Now I listen to whether a 'faith' preacher includes the words 'with persecution' because that is part of the repayment. Jesus did not promise us a life of happiness here. He said that in the world we would have big trouble — but to cheer up, he is on top of it. Jesus did not promise you a life free from trouble and pain. God promises us holiness now and happiness later. The trouble is everybody wants it the other way round. 'Please can I have my happiness now, and I don't mind being holy later.' That is not God's order. Jesus was honest. He would never let anybody come and follow him under false pretences. He would always tell them what it was going to cost, always tell them the problems. A rich young man came and he wanted eternal life. Jesus invited him to get rid of all his money and then follow him, and he could have it. But can't I have it all? Can't I have you as well as that? That is what most people want. They want Jesus on top of everything else, like the icing on the cake.

I was in Aberdeen preaching in a big theatre. A very attractive girl, about twenty-five years of age, came forward and she was sobbing and upset. She said, 'Oh David, I'm so frustrated. I want to be a Christian. You talk about loving Jesus —I want to. I have gone forward at every evangelistic meeting in Aberdeen for eighteen months; I've been counselled; I've been to classes; I've done the course. Nothing has happened. Nothing has changed. I'm beginning to doubt if there's anything in it.' I thought: now here is a situation that needs the wisdom and discernment of the Holy Spirit, and he gave it to me. I looked her in the eye and said, 'Who are you living with?'

'Oh,' she said, 'I'm living with a young man and I love him very much and he loves me.'

I asked, 'Are you married?' She said that she was not.

I continued, 'Are you living as if you were married?'

'Yes.'

'Why aren't you married?'

'Well, he doesn't want to be. He says it's only a bit of paper and as long as we love each other that's all that matters.'

I said, 'So if he walked out on you tomorrow he's not breaking any promises?'

'No,' she agreed, 'but he won't, he loves me too much.'

I said, 'Then I'll tell you the answer to your problem. You've got a very difficult choice to make. Which man do you want to live with, Jesus or that young man? You can't live with them both. Jesus doesn't join in with an arrangement like that. So which is it to be? I wish I could make the decision for you. I can't. You've got to make it, and it's a hard one, but that's your choice.'

She was angry and said, 'None of the others told me I had to do that.'

'That is why you are not getting anywhere,' I explained.

It would be lovely if I could tell you that she was converted on the spot and went away rejoicing. She didn't. She ran out of that theatre sobbing her heart out and my heart went with her, and it stayed with her, and I have prayed for her, and I wonder whether I will ever again meet that girl and find out if she made the right choice — but, you see, it is for lack of that kind of honesty that we produce 'cheap' Christians. Everybody had told her to believe, but not to repent. Don't get baptised unless you have really repented, not just professed repentance, because baptism is to be the climax of your repentance.

That is what we are to do for ourselves. Let us turn to what we are to do for others. Jude mentions three groups: those who are still wavering between the true faith and what these other teachers are saying; those who are on the verge of falling for it and going into it; and those who have got right into it and have been contaminated by it. We have a duty to these three groups. Notice that we are still not talking about the false teachers themselves, we are talking about those who are their victims.

First there are those who are wondering if there is something in it, those who are wavering, who are saying it sounds good, and they quote the Bible (because you can prove anything from the Bible if you are learning core bits of it). You have a solemn duty of love to talk to those in that group, and talk them out of it —but as you talk to them, do it with gentleness and kindness, not with harshness. Isn't that simple?

Aquila and Priscilla were great at this. They heard a preacher called Apollos and he was a bit off. He was good as far as he went. He knew the scriptures, but he was a little haywire on baptism and on the Holy Spirit. Those were two doctrines he did not fully understand. So what did Aquila and Priscilla do? They did not do what you and I do — go home and roast preacher for lunch! Instead of having roast preacher for lunch, have the preacher for roast lunch! Aquila and Priscilla had the right attitude. They were kind and gentle.

The second group, those just about to go that way — what should you do with them? More drastically, snatch them from the flames before they get burnt. The Lord will tell you how to snatch them, but it is more than just talking. If you saw a little child crawling towards the fire without a fireguard and then stretching out his hand to the flames, what would you do? Talk? Never! If you loved that child, you would grab it, and we are to do that when we see someone about to fall. The Lord will give you wisdom. We are not justifying inquisition, we are saying there is a time to act rather than just talk.

The third group are those who have got right into it and are contaminated. Jude teaches us that this is the riskiest situation because you can get contaminated if you are not careful. You must go in with love for the sinner and hate for their sin. If once you condone what they are doing, if once you get mixed up in it, you won't rest with them. You have got to go in with such a love for them and such a fear of being contaminated by them that you are afraid of their stained underwear. I am translating the Greek literally. The word means the under-vest that people wear, and the word 'stained' is used of vomit, excrement and disease. In the Old Testament such garments had to be burned. It is almost as if God was saying beware of AIDS and herpes. Be scared of any contamination whatever. Do not give them up. Show them mercy, which means give them more than they deserve. Treat them better than they deserve. You receive mercy, give them mercy with the hope that you might save them. Now this is very practical, isn't it? It is advice of love. Do not write off people who have got into false teaching. Love them. Remember how patient God was with you until you got the Bible right. Remember how he did not say: I'll treat you justly — he said, 'I will give you mercy,' and we have got to pass mercy on. Blessed are the merciful for they shall obtain mercy.

4

LOOKING TO THE FUTURE
Read 24 – 25

Jude does not leave his readers with the impression that he is setting an impossible task. How can anyone stand in such a situation with false teaching pressing in and people getting contaminated all around? How can we stand? How could I keep myself in the love of God in all that? The answer is that there is someone who is able to keep you from stumbling. Fix your eyes on the Lord. Realise that he can hold you safe.

Now there is a proper balance in all this. I know absolutely that he is able to keep me, but only if I will let him — only if I keep myself in his love. He has the ability to keep me from stumbling, but I must give him the opportunity to use his ability. It is no use just singing 'He is able to keep that which I've committed unto him against that day' if you are not letting him keep you! His ability must be matched by an opportunity, and if I do not keep faith with him, how can he 'keep'? That is the balance of scriptural teaching. That is why Jude teaches in this letter both, 'Keep yourselves in God's love . . .'; and that he, 'is able to keep you from falling . . . .' I am absolutely convinced that God is able to keep you from stumbling, but I am not convinced that you won't stumble! Do you follow me? Why not? Perhaps because you won't *let* him keep you from stumbling; you may not *keep* yourself in the love of God. Do you follow me now? It is a lovely truth that God is able to keep what I have committed to him, but in the same context, every time, there is something about keeping the faith on our side, trusting him to keep us. You cannot keep yourself but he can keep you if you are willing. He is able when I am willing. That is all there is to it, which means that every Christian, including myself, is exactly as holy as we are willing to be.

God is not only able to keep you from stumbling, he is able to make you perfect. I wonder if you have the faith for that — and not just 'one day'. He could keep you perfect today, if you will let him — and present you without fault. I cannot get over it — that God is able to make John David Pawson a perfect man without any fault! It would take my wife even more faith than I have to believe that. Bless her, she was once asked, 'What's the secret of your happy marriage?' and she said, 'Simple, we're both in love with the same man.' She was not making a very holy statement, but it was truthful. I thank God it was some years ago! Me, perfect? He is able, but am I willing? He can do it, but that doesn't say he will. God doesn't like to leave a job half done. He has begun a good work in me but he won't be happy until it is complete. He is waiting for me to say, 'Do it Lord, as soon as possible.' Normally the flesh says, 'Lord, make me holy but not just yet.'

I used to be a real fan of Richmal Crompton's 'William' books. My favourite chapter was 'William gets Converted'. William went to Sunday school one day, and a lady with cherries in her hat preached most fervently. William knew the time had come to leave sin behind, be converted, and become a true believer. It is a marvellous story. He decides that he is going to leave all his wrongdoing, all his dirty tricks, all his playing truant behind, then he just remembers that there are a few things that he hasn't done yet. So he says 'Tomorrow night, I'll do it,' and he gets up the next morning with a feeling of excitement and he doesn't know why. Then he remembers — he is going to do all the sins that day he has always wanted to do. He goes out and paints the cat green, smashes windows and locks the cook in the kitchen. He does everything he has always wanted to do and the whole day is one glorious adventure. Coming home at night he sees there is a policeman walking into the house— the next-door neighbour is coming, with a stream of other people. He realises the time has come, and the next scene is a very painful one! So he goes to bed and thinks, 'Ah well, I'm leaving it all behind tonight. Tomorrow I'm going to live the sinless life.' As he drifts off to sleep he thinks, 'But I didn't do that' —as he remembers something else he had always wanted to do . . . . It is a classic exposure of the human heart. 'Lord, make me holy, but not just yet.'

God is able to do it. He has the ability to present you in his presence faultless, without shame. That does not mean he will; there will be many Christians who will stand in his presence embarrassed and with shame that they did not let him do it. We are told that. Those who let him do his work will not only stand without any fault, they will stand with great joy. Can you imagine a bride on her wedding morning and somebody has spilled some wine down the front of the wedding dress. The stain won't come out and she has to turn up at the wedding with that great mark right down the dress. Furthermore, she has had a bad attack of acne in the last two weeks, so she has spots and she is embarrassed at her wedding because she wanted to be without any spots and she wanted the most perfect dress. She had wanted to be the most beautiful bride that has ever been. That is the picture of what can happen at the Second Coming of Christ. He wants to present a bride that is spotless, without wrinkle, in the fine white linen which is the 'clothes' of the deeds of the saints.

I was asked in a school 'Why wasn't Jesus married?' and I said to the boy who asked, 'He's going to be.' The Headmaster was there, and he looked completely puzzled. He did not know his Bible. Jesus *is* going to be married! What a wedding — what a day that will be when the bridegroom comes. Who is the bride? You! Will the bride be spotty and will the dress be stained?

He is able to present you without any imperfection, without any spot (literally) and with great joy.

And now to the only God there is . . . . There is only one God. All the other 'gods' are myths. The only God is the God of the Jews and the God of Jesus Christ, and through Jesus Christ he is our Saviour. Never fall into thinking that Jesus saved us from God. It was God who saved us from Satan through Jesus. Get your theology right! To the only God, our Saviour, to whom belongs all the glory, all the majesty, all the power and authority (and not just now, it has always belonged to him and it always will) . . . . That is the God who can keep you from falling, because he is in charge of everything. Even Satan has to ask his permission before he can touch you (read the book of Job). There is no dualism in the universe. God's kingdom is over all. You cannot extend the kingdom. Do not listen to preachers who talk about 'extending' or 'building' the kingdom of God. We cannot alter it. He rules over all anyway. That is the God who wants to save you and present you faultless. He is on your side. So you could do it. You do not need to let godlessness get into you or your church —because he is able to keep us.

'Absolutely true' — that is the meaning of the word 'Amen'. You should never say 'Amen' to a prayer unless you believe it is going to come true.

EBOOKS

Most books by David Pawson are also available
as ebooks from:

amazon.com and amazon.co.uk Kindle stores.

**For details of foreign language editions
and a full listing of
David Pawson Teaching Catalogue in MP3/DVD
or to purchase David Pawson books in the** UK
please visit:
www.davidpawson.com

Email: info@davidpawsonministry.com

Chinese language books by David Pawson
www.bolbookstore.com
and
www.elimbookstore.com.tw